IMAGES
of America

CARLSBAD AND
CARLSBAD CAVERNS

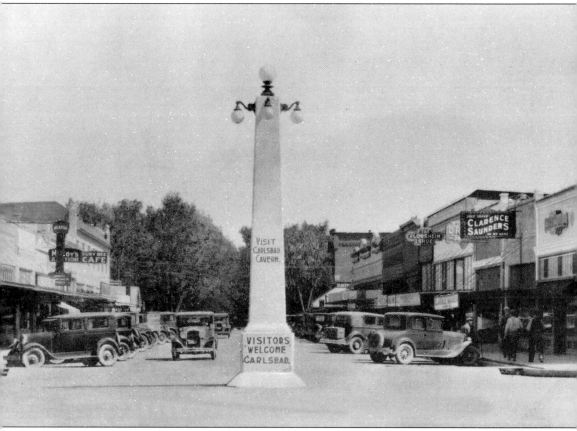

Pictured here is the tree-lined downtown business district of Carlsbad in 1924. Originally Carlsbad referred to itself as the "Pearl of the Pecos" and was called the "Cavern City" in later years. Now it is known as the "City on the Go." (Courtesy of Southeastern New Mexico Historical Society.)

ON THE COVER: In this 1924 photograph, visitors assemble in front of a grouping of stalagmites in the lower cave of what was then known as the Bat Cave, later called the Carlsbad Caverns. Explorers to the cave would be lowered two at a time by a pulley system using a metal guano-mining bucket, since elevators had not yet been installed, making it a true adventure. This photograph was taken by renowned local photographer Ray V. Davis. (Courtesy of the Carlsbad Public Library.)

IMAGES
of America

CARLSBAD AND
CARLSBAD CAVERNS

Donna Blake Birchell,
Southeastern New Mexico Historical Society,
and the Carlsbad Public Library

ARCADIA
PUBLISHING

Published by Arcadia Publishing
Charleston, South Carolina

Printed in the United States of America

Library of Congress Control Number: 2009935202

For all general information contact Arcadia Publishing at:
Telephone 843-853-2070
Fax 843-853-0044
E-mail sales@arcadiapublishing.com
For customer service and orders:
Toll-Free 1-888-313-2665

Visit us on the Internet at www.arcadiapublishing.com

*You instilled your love of history in me; I dedicate this book to
William J. Blake, the Yankee who came west to follow a dream.*

CONTENTS

ACKNOWLEDGMENTS

A huge thank-you for my dear friend and coworker Samantha Villa, without whom this book would not have been possible. When the email came asking for authors, you immediately thought of me, starting a process that has been the experience of a lifetime. Thanks Sam—you're the best!

For their patience, guidance, and enthusiasm for this project, I would like to extend a big thank you to my editors, Jared Jackson and Hannah Carney. You guys are great!

Jed Howard, for your awe-inspiring historical expertise, as well as amassing the fabulous photograph collection housed at the Society's archives, I extend my deep appreciation. I truly could not have done it without you. Unless otherwise noted, all photographs included in this volume are from the Southeastern New Mexico Historical Society archive.

Harvey Hicks, who gave me his personal blessing for this project.

Valerie Cranston, thanks for always being there.

Julie Pearson and Misty Gonzales, good friends and coworkers, your support kept me sane.

Amie McNeal, Estella Morales, Jeana Lassiter, and James Lucas—thanks for everything.

James Owens, fellow historian, although he would argue the point, thanks for keeping me on my toes and for the constant encouragement.

John LeMay, author of *Roswell* and *Chaves County*, for giving me the scoop on how this all works. Thanks for everything.

A special thanks to a dear cheerleader who has been in my corner and a rousing supporter—thank you for having my back and being so excited for me. It means the world to me.

Thanks to the rest of the hardworking staff of the Carlsbad Public Library: Cassandra Arnold, Sybil Walterscheid, Beth Nieman, Joe Rodriguez, Jane Bujac, Jeanette Bowers, Margie Mansfield, Dianne Howerton, Michelle Rodriguez, Laura Hughes, and Lanny Barnett.

Most importantly, to my sons, Michael and Justin Birchell, who have always shown unyielding support and love for their mother. You mean everything to me and I love you both with all my heart.

It is my intention to provide the most accurate and factual information possible; any errors are completely my responsibility and unintended.

INTRODUCTION

One man's perspective of desolation is another's idea of potential. Amidst the prickly-pear cactus and sagebrush, Charles Bishop Eddy, a New York cattleman, saw a desert oasis ripe for the picking, and pick he did. The beginnings of the town of Eddy were humble, but its founder had lofty dreams, envisioning a cultural mecca of the west, complete with fine dining, lodging, and theaters. His vision was of a western utopia, thus setting in motion a marketing strategy rarely seen in the 1880s. A man who possessed a hypnotic character and piercing blue eyes, Charles Eddy was able to convince others that his visions were absolute and well worth the full investment of any who would listen.

Traditionally, the birth of a town occurs when certain economic or cultural factors attract residents to the area. Eddy, on the other hand, came to fruition only after the site had been chosen and platted. An extensive promotion of Eddy's resources was then used to attract adventurous souls to the town by singing the promises of prosperity and an endless water supply. Despite the desolation of the town site, Eddy was to be built on the banks of the Pecos River, the lifeblood of the southeastern New Mexico Territory.

In his travels, Charles Eddy's promotions attracted the attentions of such notables as Patrick F. Garrett, of Billy the Kid fame, and Charles W. Greene, a newspaper owner, to invest in his venture. This odd alliance produced the Pecos Valley Irrigation and Investment Company. A wealthy Chicago cigar manufacturer, Robert W. Tansill, who had made an earlier visit to the proposed town site by schooner wagon train, was also intrigued with the area and eagerly entered into business with the newly formed company. An exhaustive promotion of their investment went international, thanks to the efforts of Charles Greene from his new home in England. Several European and eastern United States newspapers carried advertisements of New Mexico's "agricultural paradise."

Tansill insisted the newly formed town be named Eddy, to the chagrin of Charles Eddy who originally wanted to name the town Halagueno after his beloved ranch of the same name, because he believed the town would live up to the word's Spanish meaning of alluring. A vote sealed the deal and Eddy received its name. Eddy was to become Carlsbad on May 23, 1899.

Judging from size of the tent city that sprang up on the town site, Charles Eddy immediately knew the combined efforts had paid off. Not one to rest on his laurels, Eddy embarked on new efforts to bring the one instrument vital to the ultimate survival of any town: the railroad. James John Hagerman, a Canadian industrialist, wealthy mine owner, and railroad man, invested heavily in the Pecos Valley, building the area's first railroad from Pecos, Texas to Roswell, New Mexico.

Notables who hail from or lived in the area include NPR journalist Linda Wertheimer, born here in 1943, and artist Roderick Mead, who lived and died here. Bruce Cabot, born here in 1904, was the co-star of *King Kong*; Cabot's true name was Etienne Pelissier Jacques de Bujac Jr. Dan Blocker of *Bonanza* was an English and drama teacher in Carlsbad for a short time, and Andrew Gaffney, doctor and payload specialist aboard mission STS-40 of the space shuttle *Columbia*, grew up in Carlsbad.

A cowboy by the name of James "Jim" Larkin White explored the caves in the Guadalupe Mountains for years before he could get anyone interested in one particular cave he found while looking for cattle. The Bat Cave, as it was first known, was home to millions of Mexican free-tailed bats that produced great quantities of guano. Initially, the only reason for anyone to enter the cave in the beginning was to mine and sell the guano as fertilizer for California fruit crops at $90 per ton. But as White explored deeper and roused the interest of local photographer Ray V. Davis, everyone started to take notice. The cave was established as a national monument on October 25, 1923, after Robert Holley of the United States Department of the Interior toured it to see whether it was worthy of acclaim. He was awestruck by its beauty, stating in his final report, "I am wholly conscious of the feebleness of my efforts to convey the deep conflicting emotions, the feeling of fear and awe, and the desire for an inspired understanding of the divine creator's work, which presents to the human eye such a complex aggregate of natural wonders."

For years the Southeastern New Mexico Historical Society and I have wanted to produce a book illustrating the vast history of Carlsbad and its surrounding areas. It is a thrill to be able to provide this information to the public. Until now, a historical photographic representation of this magnitude of Carlsbad and the Carlsbad Caverns has not existed. We are hoping, through this book, to satisfy a need and shed light on what our region has to offer.

The people of Carlsbad are a resilient group. From the beginning, adversity has raised its ugly head, but the citizens have always found ways to overcome and surpass the troubles that may have befallen them. One man's dream of a city of opportunity has become the reality of the "City on the Go." Many events shaped Carlsbad into what it is today, as many drops of water formed the stalagmites in the Carlsbad Caverns. Carlsbad has endured many tragedies along the way, such as floods, drought, mine accidents, and economic downfalls, but has proven resilient. There still may be a few bumps along the road, but Carlsbad's future is certain to be bright.

One

OASIS ON THE PECOS

From one of the largest promotional schemes of its time, Eddy, New Mexico, was born. Charles Bishop Eddy, a charismatic visionary and cattle rancher, saw maximum potential in the acreage nestled along the sandy shores of the Pecos River. He established his ranch, which he named Halagueno, in the area around 1881 as headquarters for the Eddy-Bissell Cattle Company, on land that was still part of the famed Jingle-Bob ranch of John S. Chisum.

The stone structure that the Eddys built in 1886 just north of today's Carlsbad was the only house for 70 miles north and 100 miles south, spanning from Roswell down to the Texas border. Eddy partnered with Patrick F. Garrett (who put Billy the Kid's outlaw career to a halt), Charles W. Greene (a St. Louis newspaperman), Robert W. Tansill (Chicago cigar manufacturer), and James J. Hagerman (empire builder/railroader) to embark on the enthusiastic advertisement of the Pecos River Valley.

Water being the key to survival for a community, Eddy was touted to have the world's largest irrigation system and an inexhaustible supply of water. Brochures singing its praises were translated into French, German, and Italian. The Swiss proved to be primary investors with the English and French following close behind. Swiss and Italian farmers flocked to the area with dreams of finding the land of milk and honey.

As the investors liked what they saw, Eddy asked B. A. Nymeyer, a local surveyor, to plat out the town. All streets lined up on the points of the compass, and lots sold for $50 apiece. On September 15, 1888, Eddy was christened with the crack of a champagne bottle by Lillian Greene, daughter of Charles Greene. Ironically, a deed clause was written into every lot sold stating the purchaser could not manufacture or sell alcohol on the premises without the forfeiture of said property. The clause was so strictly enforced that the citizens of Eddy were forced to conjure up ailments to be provided with medical libations.

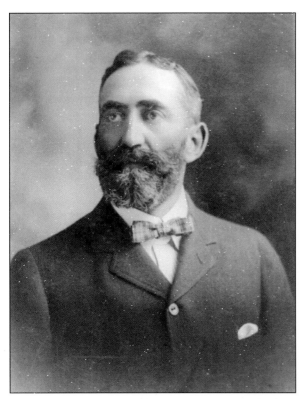

Charles Bishop Eddy was a confirmed bachelor and pitchman extraordinaire who came to the Pecos Valley from Milford, New York with his brother, John Arthur, to widen their operation in a more cattle-friendly area. Charles, shown in 1890, could be seen touring his town in a buggy hitched to a pair of matching black horses.

The Eddy House is seen in this 1907 photograph with attorney Etienne P. Bujac in the foreground. In 1991, the Southeastern New Mexico Historical Society moved the rock house from its original location in La Huerta to Heritage Park beside the flume. Each cornerstone was numbered for reconstruction at its new site.

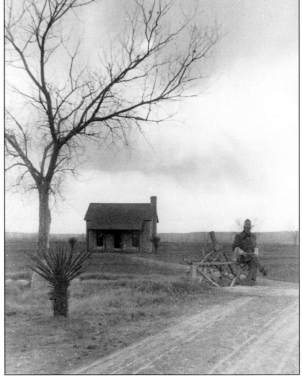

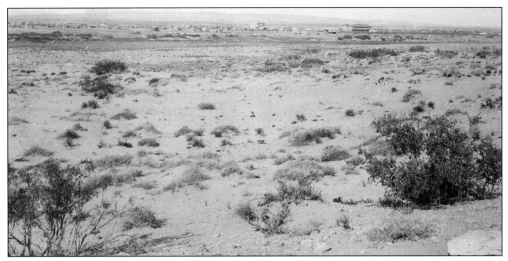

The desolation of the area was well known to the cowboys who worked this land they called Rattlesnake Flats, due to the high number of snakes living there. Cowboys had to be watchful not only for the snakes, but also the holes in which they lived, which could ruin a good horse that stepped into one.

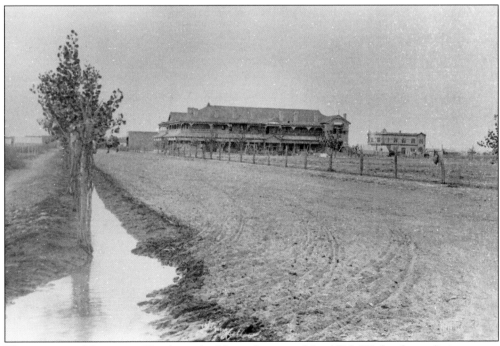

The two-story Hagerman Hotel was highly sophisticated for 1896. With a large dining room, Sunflower Club ballroom, and a fireplace in every room, the hotel was sought after by many travelers. Carpeting in the hallways, a barbershop, and bathrooms were some of the amenities provided by the English-style Hagerman.

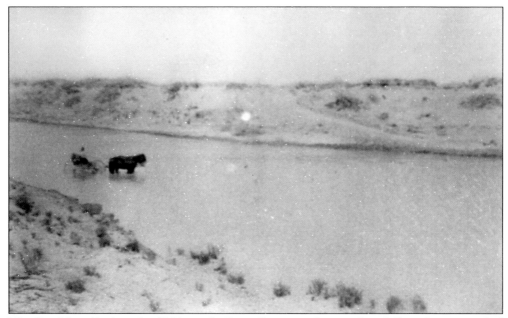

The Guadalupe Ford north of Eddy on the Pecos River was the site where Lillian Greene cracked a bottle of champagne to officially christen Eddy a town. With an expanse of 103 feet, the Pecos River at this point was only an average of two feet deep.

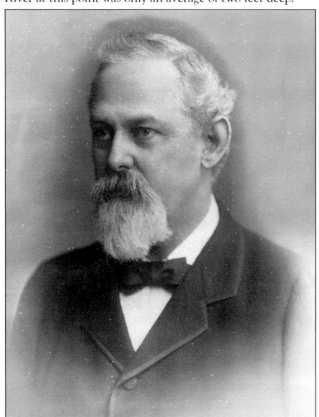

St. Louis newspaperman Charles W. Greene first encountered Charles B. Eddy in a chance meeting as he was traveling through New Mexico gathering data. After moving to England, Greene became Eddy's greatest international promoter by submitting advertising that sang the town's praises in many foreign newspapers.

James John Hagerman was heralded as an empire builder and railroad man. He was living in Colorado managing his mining ventures when Robert W. Tansill introduced him to Charles Eddy as a possible investor. He was reportedly so impressed by the area that he initially invested $40,000 in Eddy's dream.

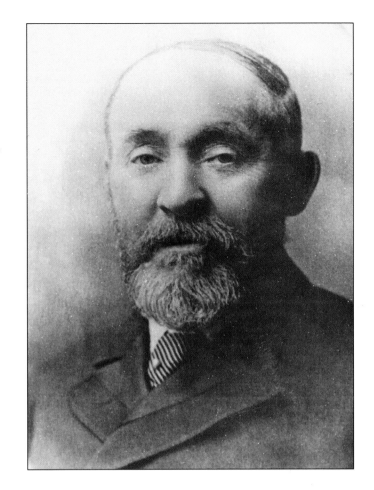

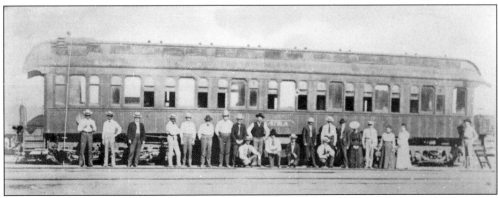

The *Alura* was the first Pullman sleeper car from the railroad built by J. J. Hagerman. Hagerman left Eddy and bought the Jingle-Bob Ranch of John S. Chisum. A feud prompted both men to leave the area. Hagerman wrote in a letter, "Our attitude is hurting New Mexico, and I will make you a proposition. If you will quit lying about me, I will quit telling the truth about you."

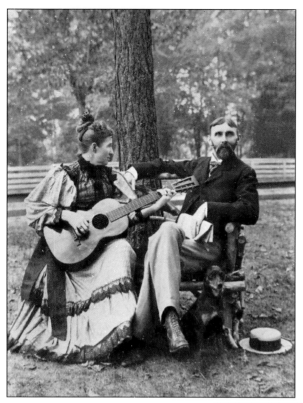

Chicago 5¢ Punch cigar manufacturer Robert Weems Tansill met Charles Eddy in Colorado Springs, where he lived. Tansill remained in Carlsbad until his death in 1902. He provided financial and managerial support for the Carlsbad Irrigation Project and believed the curative elements of the waters at the Carlsbad Springs were the same as the Bohemian springs of Karlsbad, Czechoslovakia, which he frequented.

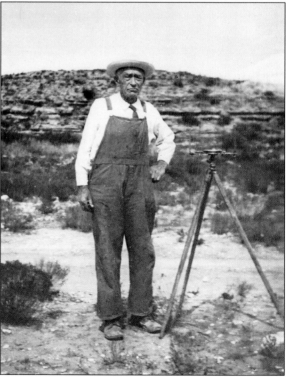

B. A. Nymeyer is shown in this 1923 photograph with his tripod at the ready. Nymeyer was an engineer, lawyer, and early surveyor of both Eddy and its sister city, Phenix, as well as the irrigation works. The "Garden Spot of New Mexico," as Eddy was described in local newspapers, was ready to be inhabited. Nymeyer's family was one of the first five farmers to take water out of the main canal to grow sorghum.

Francis G. Tracy Sr. was a pioneer, irrigation expert, hardware store owner, and writer. His writings provide much of the early history of the area. Tracy was responsible for planting the first peach orchard and experimenting with Egyptian cotton in the Pecos Valley. Members of his family still live in Carlsbad.

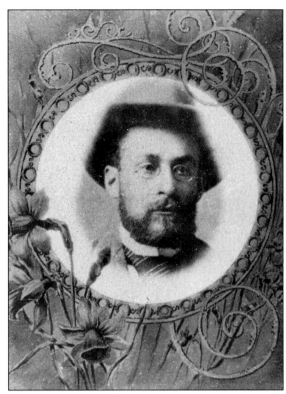

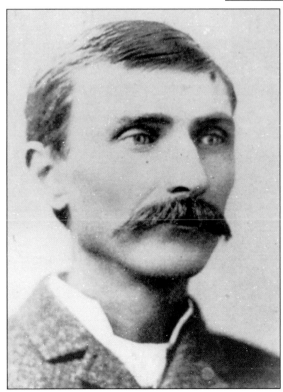

Patrick F. Garrett, buffalo hunter, businessman, lawman, and customs agent, wore many hats before and after his notorious killing of Billy the Kid. Partnering with Charles B. Eddy in the irrigation project, Garrett was able to fulfill a dream. Unfortunately, his luck did not hold later in life, as he slipped deeply into debt from gambling and started drinking heavily.

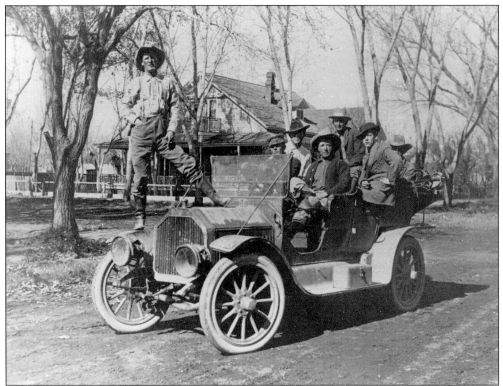

Eddy's first doctor and surgeon, Dr. Frederick Doepp (in the driver's seat), shows off the town's first Franklin automobile. Identified passengers include Earl Matheson in the back right seat, Had James with his hand on his hip, Frank James in the back left seat, and Dolph Lusk standing on the fender.

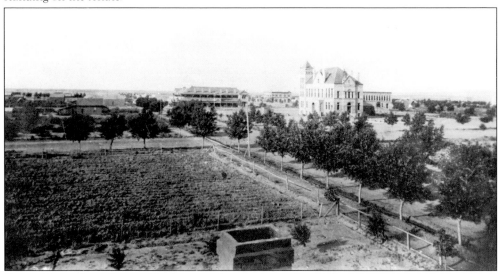

Canon Street (later Canyon) looking south is shown in this 1890 photograph by the town's first professional photographer, a Mr. Stringfellow. The posts are cottonwood saplings brought to town by Eddy. Set 15 feet apart along the four main streets of Eddy, these trees were fiercely protected by paid night watchmen from marauding burros who threatened to eat them on a regular basis.

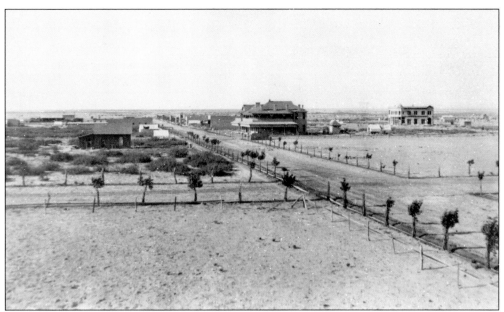

Ditch systems were hand-dug along the streets to water the new cottonwoods. Due to the severe sandstorms that often erupted in the area during the spring and fall, these ditches would have to be re-excavated. The cottonwood posts were the only visible guides for the unlucky traveler who was unfortunate enough to be caught out in one of these storms.

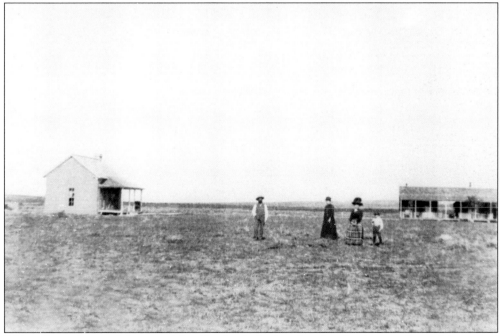

Eddy is shown here with his sister Mary Fox (in the hat) and nephew Littleton in front of the second Eddy Ranch built in La Huerta, north of town. Mary Fox was an enthusiastic hunter and reported to be a good shot. The desolation of the overgrazed valley is obvious in this 1888 photograph.

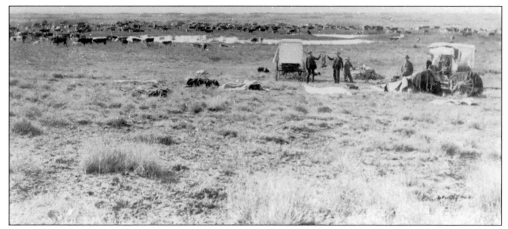

This wagon train of settlers is pictured outside of Eddy at the San Simon Range. The men proudly show off their rabbit kill. The San Simon sink was named after a large geographical depression in the area that provided protection from the severely cold weather for cattle. Obtaining grazing rights with no north-south boundaries gave them access to one million acres stretching from the Pecos River eastward to Texas by 1902.

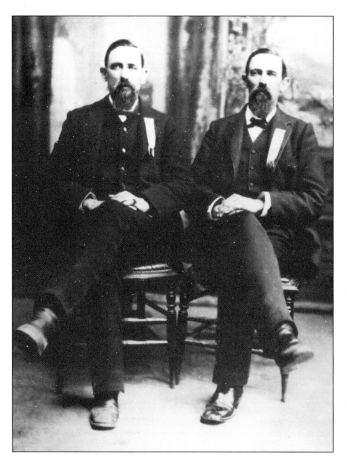

Texas-born Claiborne "Clabe" Merchant, shown here with his twin brother, John, served as a colonel in the Confederate army during the Civil War. He partnered with James H. Parramore in 1882 to start the San Simon Ranch, created in 1898, which spanned nearly all of southeastern New Mexico. The ranch house burned in 1936 and was replaced with an adobe structure boasting 20-inch-thick walls.

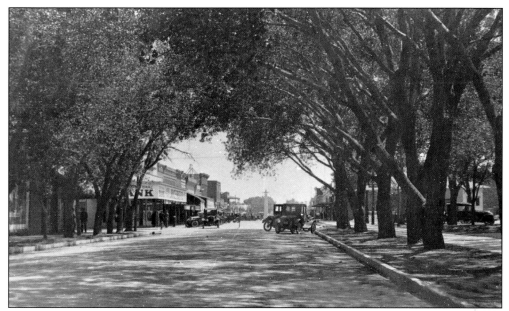

Carlsbad's business district flourished, as seen in this 1924 Leck Studio photograph. The cottonwoods had grown into trees that provided much-needed and appreciated shade for the citizens. Many of the original 6,000 cottonwoods lived to be well over 100 years old. Charles Eddy had the trees planted in double rows along the major roads of Eddy.

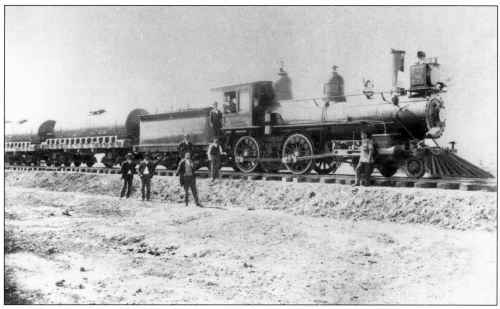

The *Pea Vine* connected Eddy with Pecos, Texas, and Roswell. On January 10, 1891, the citizens of Eddy sent Hagerman a wire message reading "We express our thanks through the subtle agency of the clouds. . . None of the notable achievements of your life are greater than this, which has changed the wilds of the mesas and the loneliness of the desert to the peaceful and prosperous agriculture and fruit growing country."

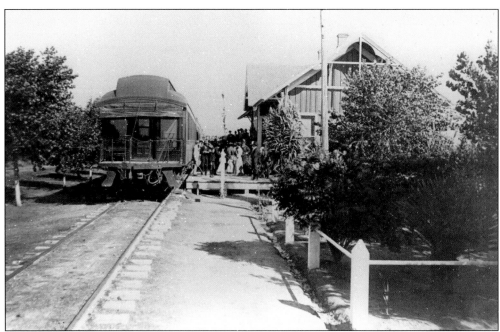

This 1912 photograph shows the Malaga railroad station with James J. Hagerman's private railroad car, the *Hesperia*, ready to be loaded with more investors. Hagerman invested over $3 million of his own money in the Pecos Valley before moving to Roswell, where the neighboring town of Hagerman was named in his honor. He passed away in September 1909 while vacationing in Milan, Italy.

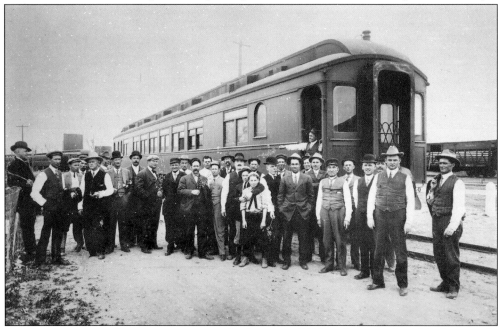

A railroad excursion of prospective investors for the town of Eddy is shown in this 1912 photograph. Groups such as these were often shuttled to the area by J. J. Hagerman, by means of his private railroad car. The investors would be wined and dined along the way, and often fed with the fruits of the valley.

Two

PHENIX RISING

Started as a place for Eddy residents to sell alcohol, Phenix had high hopes. From the tent city rose stores, restaurants, a theater, an opera house, gambling houses, and several saloons. The saloons, owned by locals and sheriffs, soon attracted outlaws, prostitutes, and gamblers. John Wesley Hardin, Clay Allison, Martin M'Rose, and Tom "Black Jack" Ketchum were all reported to have frequented the facilities. Reports of Billy the Kid visiting are false, however, since Phenix was established in 1892, some 11 years after he was killed by Patrick Garrett in Fort Sumner.

Sheriff Dave Kemp was no stranger to both sides of the law, having been accused of murder as a teenager. Kemp was the owner of saloons not only in Phenix, but also in the sister suburb of Wolftown. The tent city of Wolftown was built directly on the ruts of the road back to Eddy from the north. Workers would either have to stop or go out of their way to completely avoid the establishment to continue on their way.

The *Eddy Argus*, a local newspaper, reported: "Some of our citizens went to Black River, and some got no farther than Phenix, and there remained deeply immersed in the history of the four Kings, or muddled their brains attempting to solve the mysteries of the Anheuser-Busch combination."

As gambling and prostitution flourished in Phenix, so did crime. Decent citizens were unable to patronize the other attractions Phenix had to offer without being accosted by drunks and half-naked women. This situation caused an outcry from the townsfolk. Deputy Dee Harkey, previously a saloon owner himself, was hired to eliminate the rough elements from the town, a job he took seriously. Jeered by the women of the brothel and its owner, Ed Lyell, Harkey began enforcing the Edmunds Act by arresting many of the ladies and their pimps repeatedly. Defeated, the Phenix group left for Globe, Arizona in 1895 with great fanfare as their band played a rendition of "Bonaparte's Retreat" in Harkey's honor.

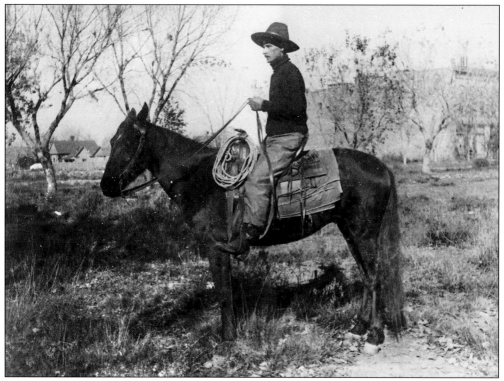

Dee Harkey, cowboy, butcher, lawman, and author of *Mean as Hell*, was the nightmare of Phenix businessmen. Hired to clean out what the town called pests, Harkey quickly became the thorn in the side of many saloon and brothel owners while raising the ire of sheriff Dave Kemp. He accomplished his goal as a constable under Cicero Stewart.

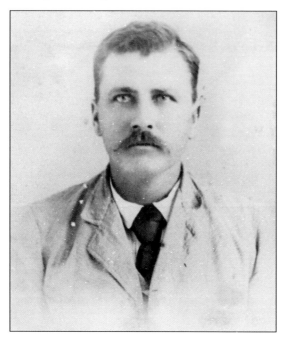

Pictured in this 1894 photograph, sheriff and saloon owner Dave Kemp was a dashing figure in the area, but trouble followed him like a shadow. The *Eddy Argus*, a local newspaper, said his only vice was chewing gum although he would later be accused and acquitted of the murder of rival sheriff candidate Les Dow. He died of a heart attack in 1935 at the age of 73.

James Leslie "Les" Dow made a fast enemy of Dave Kemp by arresting him for calf rustling as a detective for the Texas-New Mexico Cattle Raiser's Association. Kemp later returned the favor by arresting Dow for rustling 23 of his cattle. Dow convinced the court that brand tampering had occurred and was released. The bad blood between the two would lead to Dow's eventual death.

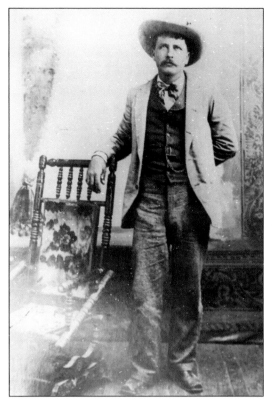

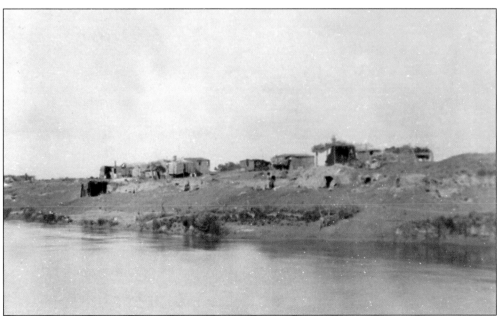

Little Chihuahua, a Mexican-American village, was originally dug into the west banks of the Pecos River, but with the arrival of the railroad, the general manager forced the entire population of 12 families to move to the east side to accommodate the tracks. Small wood and adobe shacks were built to house the residents.

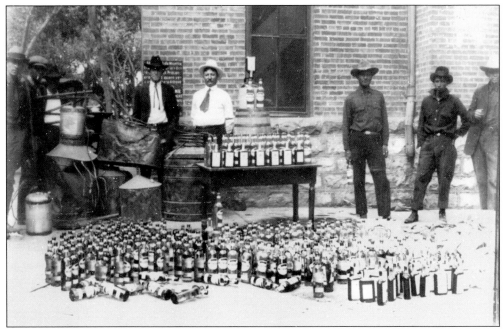

Confiscated stills and bottles of whiskey were commonplace in early Eddy. The drugstores would order in whiskey by the casks, filling bottles only for medicinal purposes, of which the citizens of Eddy were allowed to write their own prescriptions. Pharmacists were called to task about this practice and fined heavily if convicted.

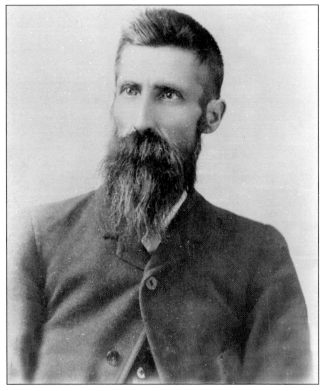

As Dee Harkey enacted the Edmunds Act on the citizens of Phenix, he would deliver them to Judge A. A. Freeman's Fifth Judicial District Court of the New Mexico Territory in Socorro. By 1895, Ed Lyell, the leader of the Phenix group, was told by Judge Freeman all charges would be dropped in exchange for leaving the area. The contingent moved to Globe, Arizona 15 days later.

Four dandies of the town of Carlsbad pose in front of Leck's Grocery and Pool Room, which was a popular spot for gentlemen to gather in 1902. Before moving west, owner William Leck received minor wounds in the Battle of Gettysburg in the 5th Pennsylvania Cavalry. He operated his store on the 200 block of South Canyon Street for two decades.

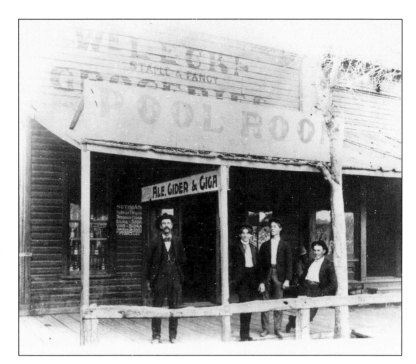

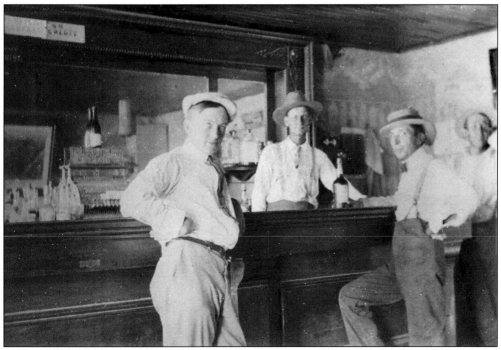

The Loving Saloon, owned by Fred Montgomery, was located 12 miles south of Eddy in the small suburb of Loving. Loving was named in memory of cattleman Oliver Loving, who was attacked and mortally wounded a few miles from the hamlet. Loving did not have the same restrictions as Eddy on alcohol, but it was a good distance from Eddy, unlike Phenix, which was only a mile away.

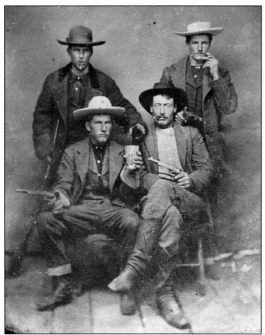

Some believe the man standing in the left of this photograph to be Billy the Kid, but after much debate, it is thought more likely to be Bob Speaks. Standing to the right is Jim Jones. Seated, from left to right, are John Jones and Buck Powell, all members of the Seven Rivers Warriors gang. The Joneses were personal friends of Billy the Kid.

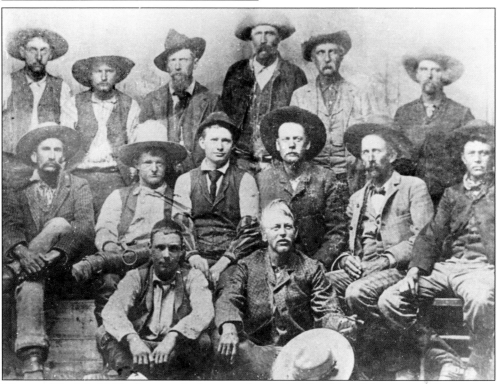

Thomas "Black Jack" Ketchum worked as a cowboy in the Guadalupe Mountains before joining up with his brother Sam to rob railroads across the territory. Ketchum, the tallest man in the back row, pictured here along with members of his Guadalupe cattle drive, was ultimately hanged for train robbery in Clayton, New Mexico.

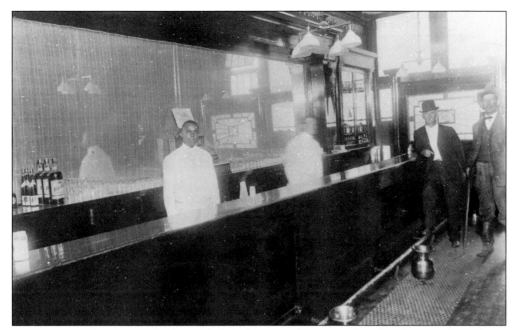

After Phenix closed and Charles Eddy left the area, the town of Carlsbad got its first saloon. Shown here is the Barfield Saloon located at 205 West Fox Street in Carlsbad, with Fred Thornton, the first black bartender. The *Eddy Argus* considered the saloon "that great curse and evil of civilization."

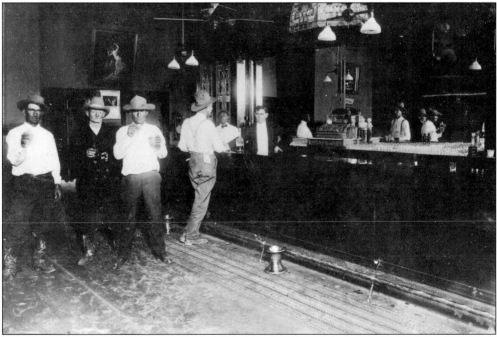

The interior of a similarly decorated saloon located at 128 S. Canyon Street, around the corner from the Barfield Saloon, is featured in this 1908 photograph. Leaded glass windows, oil lamps, and nude paintings added to the saloon's ambiance. Belle of Bourbon, Kentucky Comfort, and California claret were popular spirits during this time. This saloon later became Star Pharmacy.

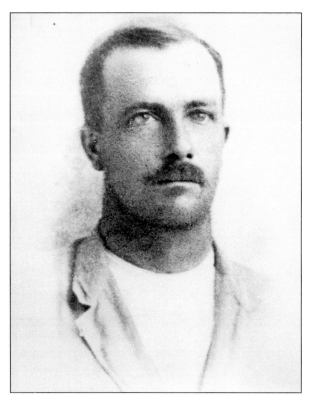

John D. Walker, featured in this 1895 portrait, was assessor before being elected for a yearlong term as sheriff in Eddy. He defeated reputed outlaw Walker Bush, who was reported to have killed seven men and was highly supported by his half-brother, Dave Kemp. Bush's defeat began the downhill swing of what was locally known as Kemp's "courthouse ring" of personally chosen deputies.

Eddy County sheriff Miles Cicero Stewart was partially responsible for bringing down the train-robbing Ketchum Gang run by Black Jack Ketchum, by engaging in a shootout with and eventually arresting Elzy Lay at Chimney Wells. Stewart lost his first bid for sheriff to Les Dow, but ironically was asked to finish his term when Dow was fatally shot.

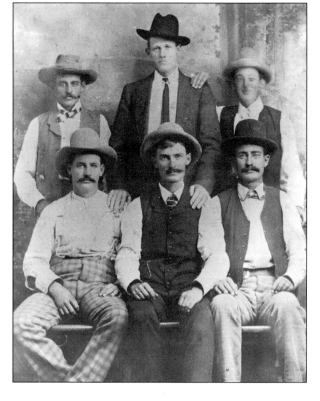

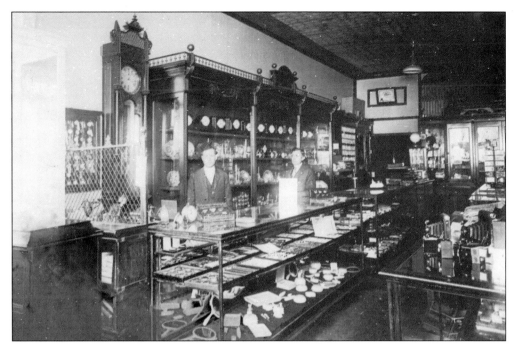

Corner Drug was the first drugstore in Carlsbad in 1914, a time when coal oil mixed with sugar, molasses, or honey was used as a cure for most ailments. Turpentine and castor oil combinations acted as a diuretic, laxative, stimulant, and tonic. Strychnine sulfate is highly toxic, but was widely used by early druggists. Whiskey was still the most favored prescription in the county.

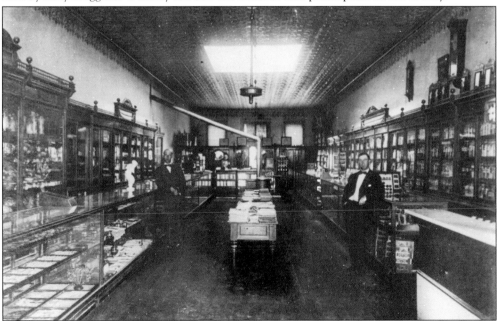

Tin ceilings and a potbellied stove were prominent features of the Eddy Drug Store. The drugstore was a place to find many unusual items to purchase. Those suffering a cough were given the syrup of squill (which is essentially rat poison), paregoric, peppermint water, lavender water, and wild cherry syrup.

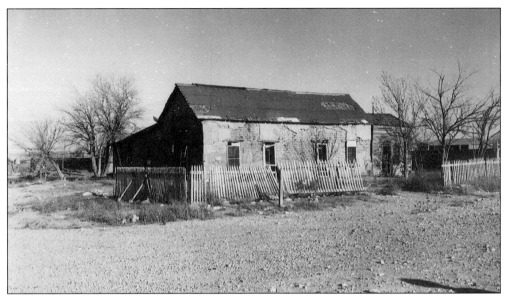

The last surviving structure of Phenix is pictured here shortly before it was torn down in 1989. This building was still occupied until only a few years before it came down. Rumors of gold buried around the house attracted many treasure hunters, only to be disappointed in their efforts. Surviving the many mysterious fires that plagued Phenix, the building was thought to have housed a saloon.

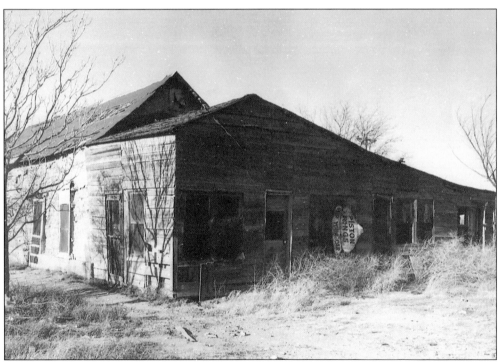

Local legend tells of a tunnel built and maintained by the gentlemen of Eddy in order to anonymously visit Phenix, otherwise known as Jagtown. Although no evidence has ever been found, older locals will swear to its existence. This building contained several rooms, six outside doors, and outside adobe walls measuring 17 inches thick. Thwarted efforts were made to preserve the building.

Three

LIFEBLOOD OF THE VALLEY

It is said Patrick Garrett's dreams of irrigated land were induced, ironically, by Billy the Kid, who is reported to have told the lawman, "Why waste your time riding these damn ranges when you could run some of this water and grow crops and sell lots?"

The Desert Land Act of 1877 encouraged the economic development of the arid land by allowing a married couple to purchase it at $1.25 per acre. The only provision was the land must be irrigated and cultivated. Charles Eddy and Patrick Garrett took advantage of this offer and formed the Pecos Valley Land and Ditch Company in 1887 for the purpose of developing an irrigation system. The Pecos Irrigation and Investment Company, with Patrick Garrett as its vice president, soon succeeded this corporation. The Pecos Valley Irrigation and Improvement Company went into receivership in 1898, with Tansill appointed receiver, and was reorganized by Francis Tracy in 1900.

A major flood raged through the town, taking with it the newly constructed wooden flume, dams, and bridges. With the help of Hagerman and Tansill, the irrigation system was rebuilt with a concrete flume in 1903. The next year saw more flooding, which threw the irrigation company into bankruptcy.

As James Hagerman's disillusionment with the Pecos Valley grew, the partnership with Charles Eddy dissolved and each man eventually left the area, never to return. With the irrigation system in shambles, almost all hope was lost for the tiny town of Carlsbad. As it happened, a former Rough Rider living in Carlsbad made a personal appeal to Pres. Theodore Roosevelt on the town's behalf; by 1906 the United States Reclamation Service was authorized to take over the Carlsbad Irrigation Project. Through this action, New Mexico acquired its first successful reclamation project, one of the earliest in the nation. The sale price was $150,000, about 10¢ on each dollar originally spent. The 145 miles of ditches and both dams were rebuilt in 1909.

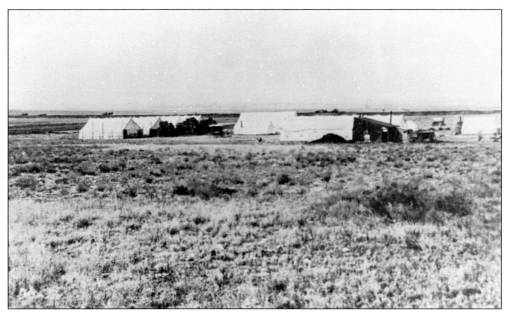

Rock Dam (now Avalon Dam) construction camp was southeast of the dam and canal construction, which can be seen in the background in March 1890. The tent city was to house irrigation laborers advertised for by W. C. Bradbury and Company. They offered $1.75 a day or $25 a month with board included to any American man. When too few white workers showed up, workers were recruited from Little Chihuahua, South Texas, and Mexico.

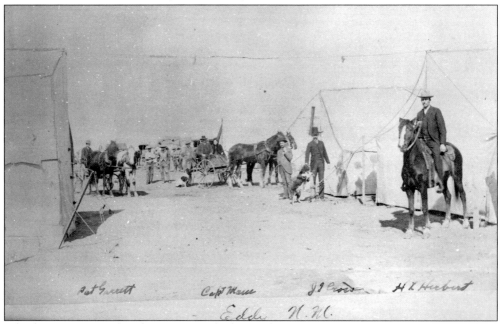

Patrick Garrett, seated in the wagon on the left, is shown in this 1889 photograph of Bradbury's headquarters. W. C. Bradbury, with his gun and $500 dog, kept the local company hotel supplied with all kinds of small game. A Massachusetts native, Bradbury first came out west for his health, possibly ailing from tuberculosis. He worked in Colorado, Wyoming, Idaho, and New Mexico as a contractor, builder, and rancher.

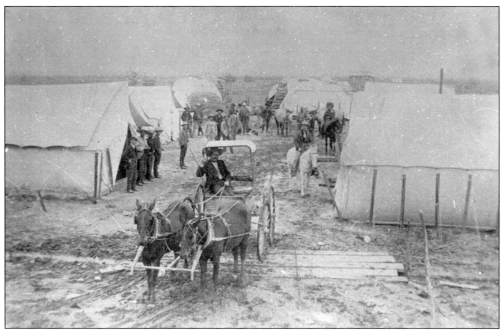

W. C. Bradbury's construction camp included a commissary for the approximately 180 workers who lived onsite. It was run by Jim Warren, who estimated a half-ton of candy was consumed by the flume workers every month. The tent town was called Flume Town by the locals. Also at the camp was a blacksmith shop, a harness shop, boarding tent, and immense dining tent.

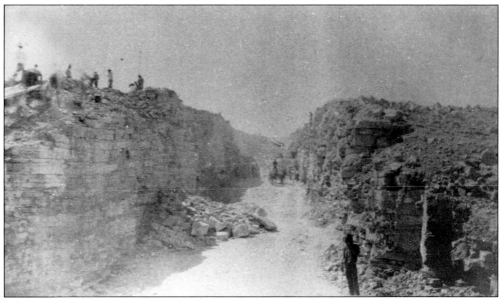

The main cut at Rock Dam (Avalon) carries water to the head gates of the large main canal, pictured here in a Stringfellow photograph taken in March 1890. Rock Dam was one of the first rock fill dams with an impervious earth fill facing ever constructed in the United States for irrigation purposes.

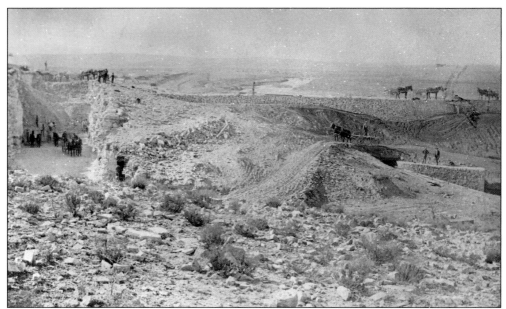

Construction of the Eddy Canal was a marvel to local citizens. After the national government took over the project in 1905, 24-foot-thick concrete diaphragm lining and rock filled canal walls were constructed. The Carlsbad Reclamation Project irrigation system was to be declared a National Landmark in 1964 as one of the most extensive private irrigation systems in the west.

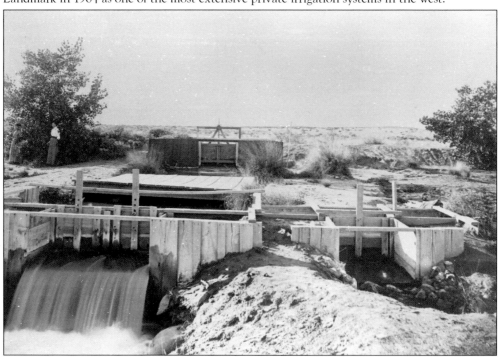

Wooden head gates of the Eddy Canal delivered the fruits of many months of hard labor to the crops of Eddy. The flume and primary canal were mostly finished before the dam was completed. The company spent $400,000 on building the canals and $90,000 on the dam. The canal was wide enough at the bottom for four teams of wagons to pass.

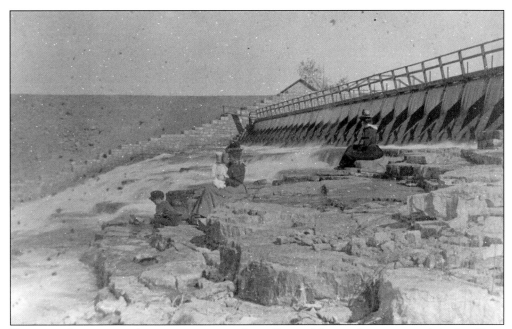

Townspeople enjoy an afternoon outing on the spillway of the newly constructed Avalon Dam, a diversion dam located 13 miles north of Eddy. The craggy banks were likened to a miniature Giant's Causeway located on the coast of Northern Ireland near Antrim. A buggy ride to Avalon Dam was considered to be one of the great pleasures of living in Eddy.

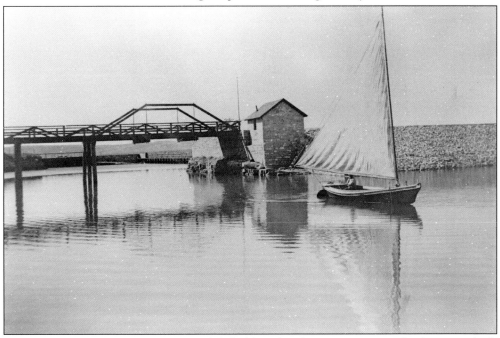

Sailing on Avalon Dam reservoir was a delightful weekend pastime in 1896. The dam was rebuilt after an 1893 flood. The *Eddy Argus* boasted Eddy had a splendid boating course, including good rowing water extending from the flume to the dam. Many of the sailboats were specially ordered and shipped 1,326 miles from Chicago.

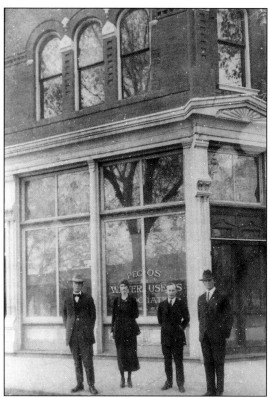

Members of the Pecos Water Users Association stand in front of the office housed in the First National Bank Building. The Carlsbad Irrigation District was headquartered in the very same building until 2007, when a pair of restaurateurs purchased the building and restored, remodeled, and returned it to its former glory.

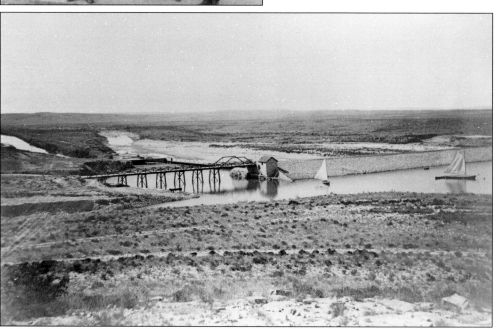

Pleasure boating was a great Sunday pastime as pictured here by the two sailboats enjoying the waters near the Avalon Dam. The dam was rebuilt in 1905 with a reinforced concrete core wall with an earth embankment on the water side and a rockfill on the downstream side, considered to be a western innovation. Captain Kinder provided sailboats for rent in 1896.

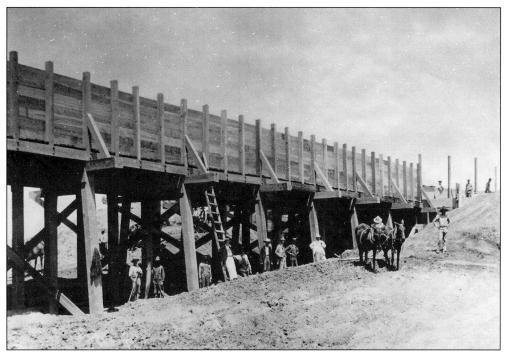

The construction of the original wooden flume near completion is shown in this 1892 photograph. The local newspaper gave updates on construction periodically, permitting the citizens of Eddy to follow the modern marvel in the making. The wooden flume was destroyed by raging floodwaters in 1893 and several high waters. It was rebuilt in concrete in 1903, and still stands today.

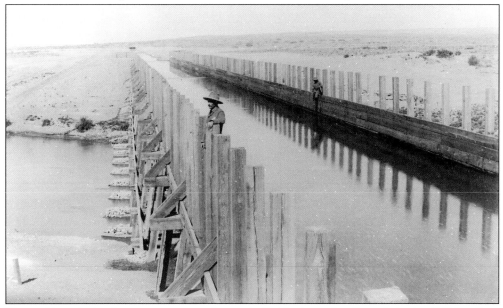

Pictured here is the first water to cross the newly finished wooden flume bringing 9,000 gallons of water per second to the parched crops of the Pecos River valley. The flume also caught the attention of the modern world as it was later given the honor of being featured in Ripley's Believe It or Not as the river that crosses itself. The water flow was about two feet deep.

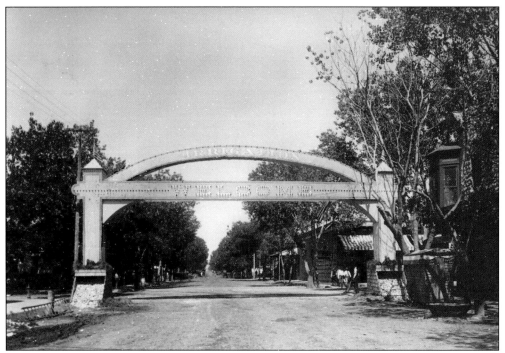

The welcome arch erected over Fox and Canyon Street for the International Irrigation Congress Conference of 1907 is shown in this photograph. The conference brought farmers, scientists, and government officials to Carlsbad to discuss advancements and management in irrigation. The world's eyes were clearly on the successes of Carlsbad's new irrigation system.

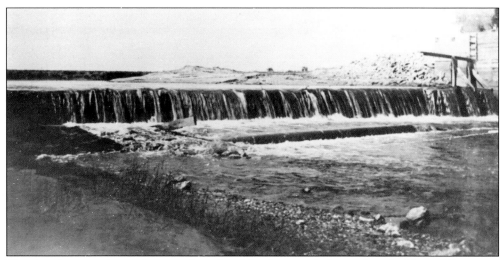

The electric power plant is shown at the right of the photograph during the rebuilding of Hagerman Dam after the 1893 flood. Hagerman built a mile-long underground flume from the dam to his original power plant at a huge cost to him. When the time came to dedicate it, the lower gates were not opened, causing the entire system to explode, sending timbers high into the air.

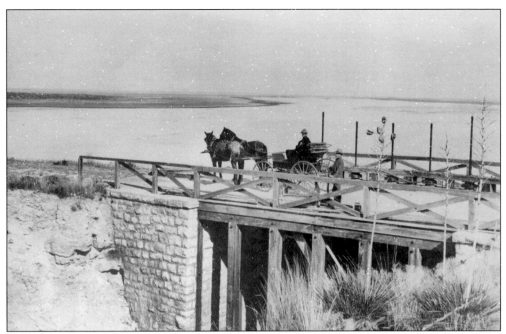

The access bridge over the head gates of Lake McMillan Reservoir located north of Eddy, now Carlsbad, is shown in this 1895 photograph. Serving as a large-volume water storage facility, holding eight times the amount of the Pecos River waters released into Rock Dam further downstream, the first of two diversion dams.

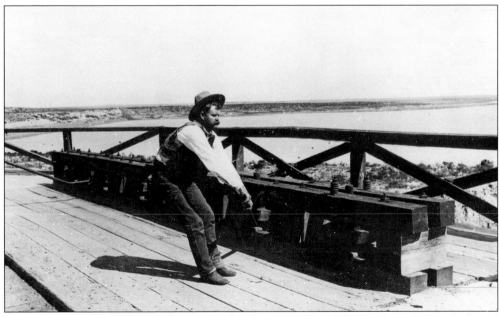

It took great strength to raise the massive head gates at the 1,686-foot-long, 52-foot-high and 30-foot-wide Lake McMillan Dam. The headworks alone cost $20,000 in 1893. There were six wooden gates, each four-by-eight-feet, with iron gates six inches thick. McMillian was called in the 1894 *Engineering Record* "the largest artificial reservoir in America and . . . one of the greatest in the world."

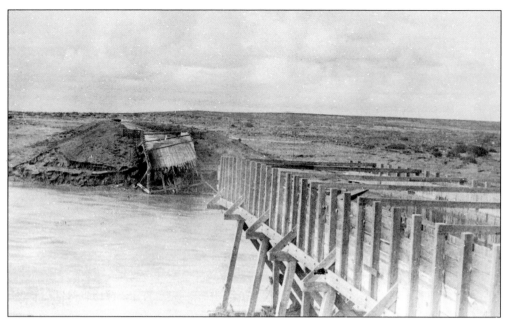

The original wooden flume was eradicated by floodwaters in 1893. Large cloudbursts originating in the mountains continued for many days, causing flash floods to roar through the upper canyons. Storm after storm soaked the land, causing a large runoff. Timbers from washed out bridges upstream took their toll on the flume and bridges downstream, causing over $125,000 in damages.

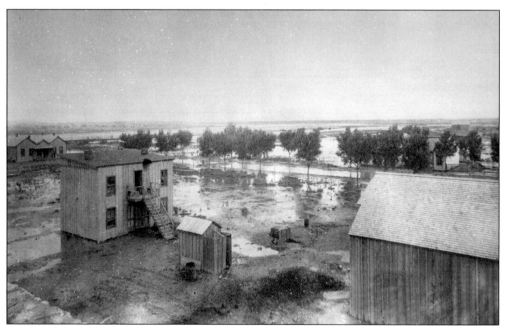

The town of Eddy was covered in foot-deep floodwaters in 1893. The three-gabled structure in the background is the first building built in Eddy, called the Eddy House. This would be the first of the 15 recorded floods in the town's history that would cause great damage and financial loss for the community. J. J. Hagerman pledged to the town that the irrigation system would be rebuilt quickly.

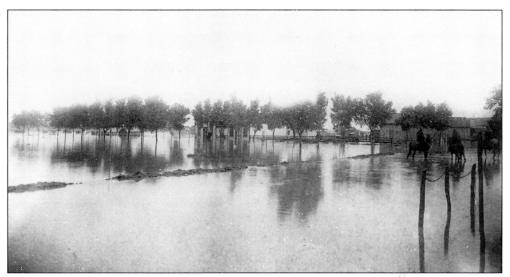

Downtown Eddy appeared to be a lake after the 1893 flood. Waters from the Pecos River overran the banks, covering the town, the railroad, and crops. Carcasses of dead cattle choked the gateways of the Avalon Dam and caused the dam to break, sending water onto the plains surrounding Eddy.

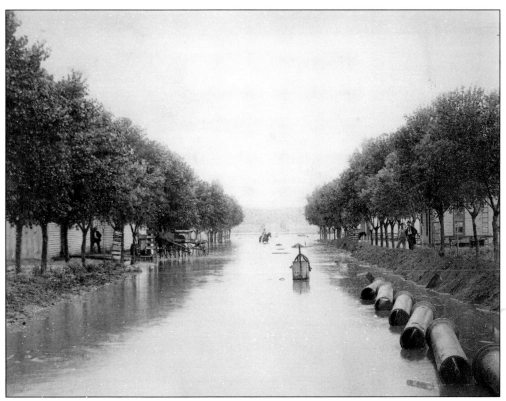

Construction of the sewer system was underway as the floodwaters ran through town. Sewer pipes lined the road waiting to be installed. Drainage would remain a constant problem for Eddy and modern-day Carlsbad. Eddy was the first town in the area to install a sewer system of any kind.

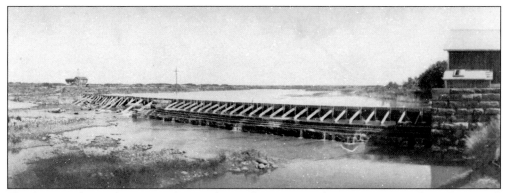

Floodwaters of 1893 threaten to destroy the newly constructed Hagerman Dam (later the Tansill Dam). Floods posed a problem for the irrigation system and citizens over the years. Many devastating floods occurred until the Brantley Dam project was completed in 1987. A 20-foot section of the dam was lost during the flood. The newspaper stated the damage "demoralized the Hagerman Dam and two Pecos River bridges."

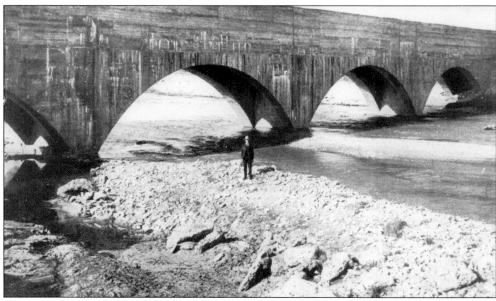

The concrete flume, which replaced the wooden version washed out in the previous floods, was completed in 1903. Although it was badly damaged, it survived the flood of 1904, which wiped out bridges, dams, and railroad tracks. The impressive structure was designed by Thomas Johnston, a former engineer with the Army Corps of Engineers.

Fishing was great sport in the early days of Carlsbad. In this 1924 photograph, two unidentified fishermen show off a prized specimen of Pecos River catfish, which weighed upwards of 75 pounds. Even larger ones have been pulled from the river over the years.

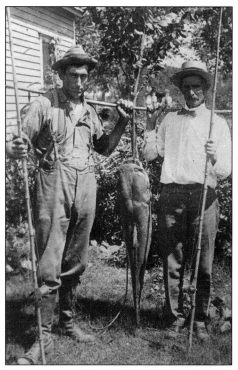

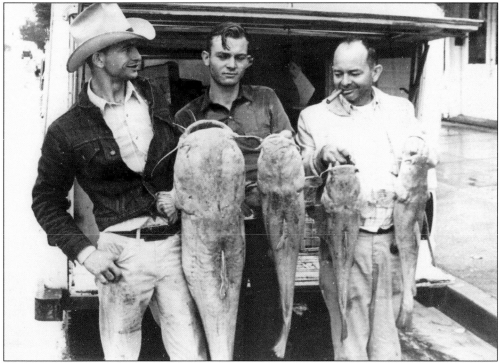

The unidentified men in this 1976 photograph seem quite happy with their catch, showing off prime examples of the range of sizes of bigmouth catfish in the Pecos River. Corn and chicken liver is used sometimes as favored bait for catfish.

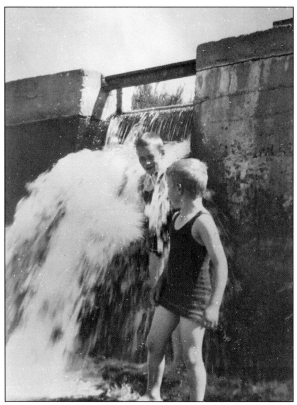

Doug and Sam Roberts cool off in the headwaters of the Carlsbad Springs in this 1909 photograph. The Carlsbad Springs were a popular area for family gatherings and picnics. The mineral content made the water soft and refreshing. As a part of Heritage Park today, the Carlsbad Springs still enjoy many visitors.

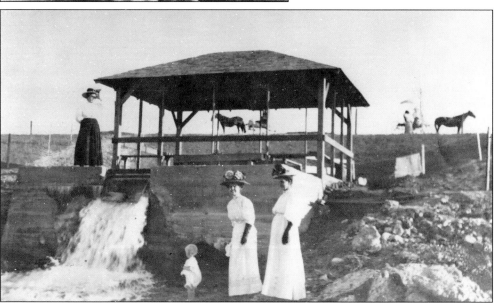

The Carlsbad Springs, which claimed to have the same qualities as the famous Karlsbad Spa waters in Czechoslovakia, attracted tubercular patients and locals alike to their healing waters. Vials of the water were sold for $1 each, and it was ritual for patients to drink the water twice a day. Many claimed they were cured by the mineral contents. The original springhouse was washed away in 1904 but has been replaced.

Four

FARMING AND RANCHING
ALONG THE PECOS

The Pecos Valley and Carlsbad have played host to many an explorer and cattle baron who followed the Pecos River. Cabeza de Vaca in 1536, Don Antonio de Espejo in 1583, Charles Goodnight and Oliver Loving in 1866, and John S. Chisum in 1868 are just a few who used the Pecos River as their guide.

Cattle drives were a common sight in the southeastern part of the New Mexico Territory. The destination for many of these cattle was old Fort Sumner to be used to fulfill government contracts, which were said to be behind the Lincoln County War.

The saga of the Goodnight/Loving Trail was fictionalized in Larry McMurtry's *Lonesome Dove*, showing a partnership that lasted beyond death. Oliver Loving and another hand named One-Armed Bill Wilson went ahead of the rest of the outfit to scout for Native American activity. They saw nothing for two days, but in Cass Draw, close to the modern-day town of Loving, they were attacked by approximately 80 Comanche. Wilson barely escaped, nearly naked, bootless, and unarmed, but Oliver Loving, who received a mortal wound in the wrist by a buffalo gun, was not so lucky. In his weakened condition, he made it to Fort Sumner for medical attention with the help of four boys he encountered near Eddy. Unfortunately, his wound was too severe, and he died. Loving's death greatly upset Charles Goodnight, who took his partner back to his home in Weatherford, Texas in a casket packed in charcoal. Goodnight saved money over the next two years and presented Loving's family with $40,000 to replace the wages they would have received if Loving had completed his journey.

Farmers flocked to the Pecos Valley with the promise of unlimited water and fertile soil. Italy, Switzerland, and Germany were well represented. The Italians established large vineyards, and the Swiss grew wheat, oats, sorghum, alfalfa, corn, and potatoes. Peaches, and later cotton, proved to be prized crops. The Pecos Valley is also known for its production of pecans, and valley apples once took first prize at the Chicago World's Fair.

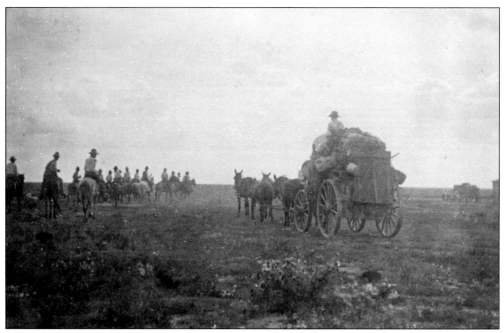

This picture shows the beginnings of a roundup with the all-important chuck wagon taking up the rear position loaded with all the supplies the cowboys will need to complete the several weeks on the trail gathering cattle. The cook, called "Cookie," was considered to be the most important and revered hand on the roundup, with the exception of the trail boss.

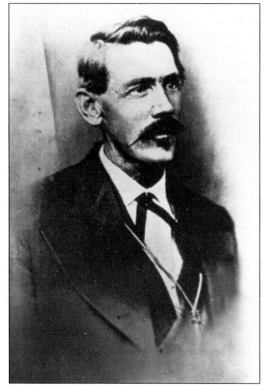

Cattle baron John Simpson Chisum was owner of the Jingle-Bob Ranch, which extended for 150 miles in southeastern New Mexico. Jinglebobs were attached to spurs next to the rowel and would drag the ground causing a jingle sound. Chisum developed earmarking unique to his cattle, by slicing a flap of ear causing it to dangle. Chisum was well liked by most, and was known never to carry a weapon.

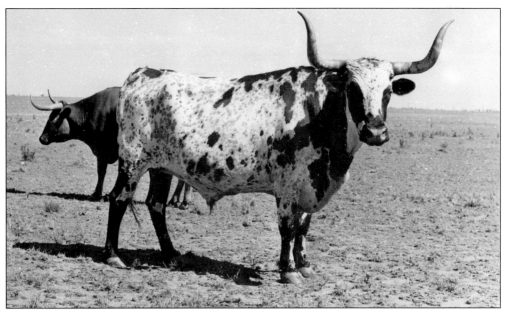

This is a typical example of the longhorn cattle John Chisum brought from Texas to the Pecos Valley in 1867. By 1872, Chisum's herd had grown to 20,000 head. He traded 2,400 for the 40-acre South Springs River ranch, 5 miles south of Roswell, which was to become the Jingle Bob headquarters.

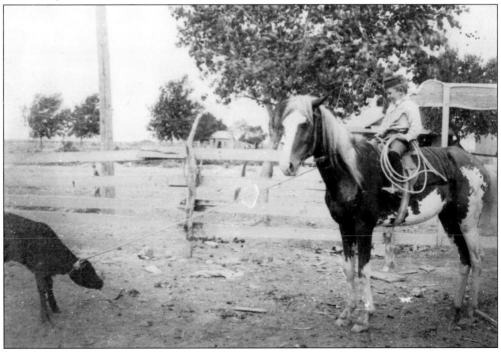

Robert "Bob" Dow, the young son of Les Dow, practiced lassoing his pet calf on their Seven Rivers ranch. The family moved to Eddy shortly after this photograph was taken. Les Dow, a saloon owner in Seven Rivers, was famous for killing outlaw Zack Light, who attempted to rob him. Dow later became sheriff of Eddy.

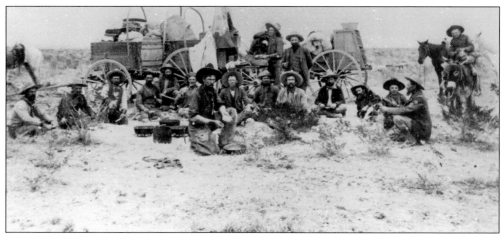

After a long day's work, cowboys would come back to the campsite ready for a good meal. Generally this meal consisted of meat, beans cooked with salt pork, unleavened biscuits or hard tack, dried fruit, and potatoes if available. No matter the temperature, a freshly brewed pot of coffee was a welcome drink.

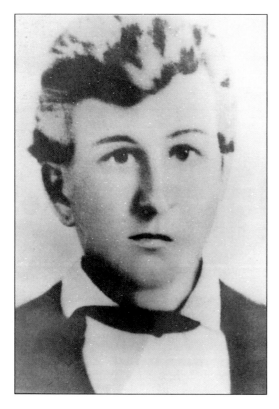

Kentucky-born Oliver Loving amassed a small herd of cattle by the start of the Civil War. The Confederate government commissioned Loving to provide beef for their soldiers and reportedly owed him between $100,000 to $250,000 by war's end. After hearing about the need for beef in Fort Sumner, he teamed up with Charles Goodnight to form the Goodnight-Loving Trail, which eventually combined with the Chisum Trail.

Charles Goodnight, who smoked 50 cigars a day and never learned to read or write, was known as a master cattleman. Cattle being his first love, he also preserved a herd of buffalo that still survives today. Goodnight dabbled in other things as well, such as newspapers and a bank, but an investment in a Mexican silver mine proved to be his financial downfall. Undaunted, Goodnight went into filmmaking.

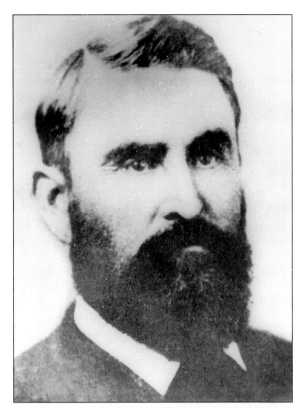

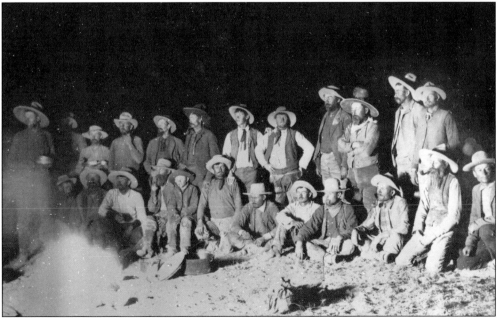

This is a rare nighttime photograph of a group of Seven Rivers cowboys gathered around the campfire at the end of a long day on the range. Ranch owners sometimes hired photographers to follow the roundup, recording cowboy and ranch life with their images. This photograph was most likely taken after flash powder was thrown into the campfire.

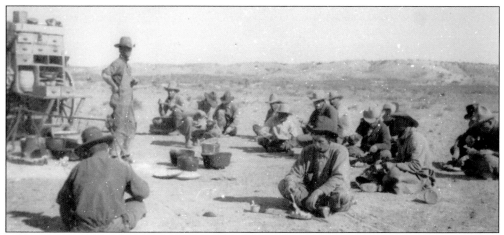

Jingle-Bob cowboys gather for a morning meal before spending the next 10 hours on horseback. A chuck wagon would haul all the food and utensils needed to make meals for the outfit of cowboys during the entire time they were out on roundup. The cook would always point the tongue of the wagon due north, and the trail boss knew which direction to head in a glance.

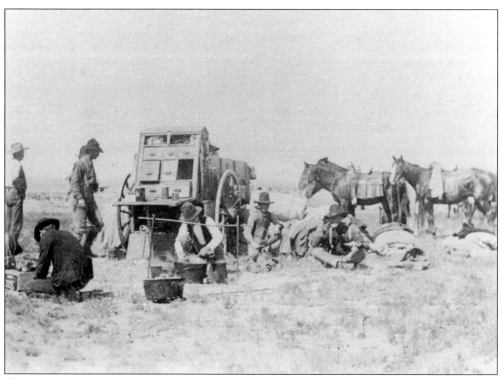

The Turkey Track Ranch crew and chuck wagon are shown at mealtime. Etiquette played a part in chuck wagon eating. It was acceptable to eat with fingers since the food was clean. Food left on the plate was an insult to the cook. Saddling a horse by the chuck wagon was not allowed, and no one ate until the cook called.

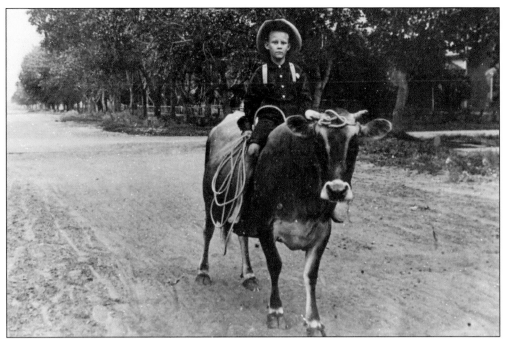

Frank and Maggig Jones's nine-year-old son Coley rides the family milk cow home in this 1909 photograph. The town of Carlsbad was blessed with a milk cow named Muley, which was allowed to roam Eddy freely because it belonged to a leading family. The local newspaper sang her praises and was rewarded by the owner with milk, cream, and butter.

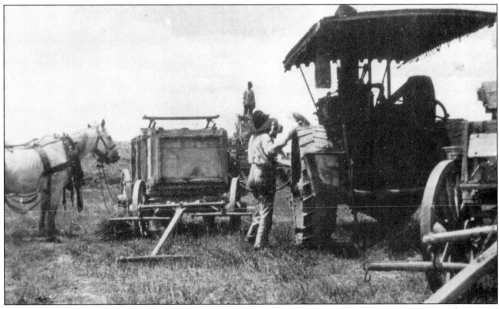

A steam traction engine and water wagon used on the Nymeyer/Ora farm, shown in this 1925 photograph, are examples of the farm equipment used in the Pecos Valley. The steam engine was a prelude to the internal combustion engine and was much more cumbersome, but it got the job done. It was self-propelled and was used to move heavy loads on roads or in plowing. They were called road locomotives.

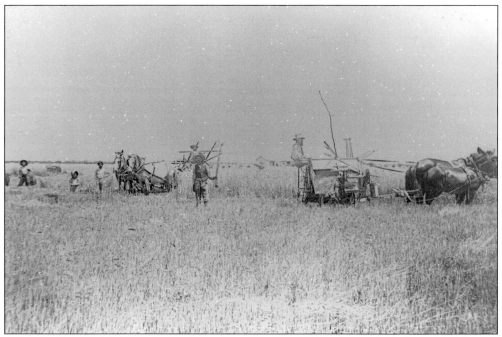

The horse-drawn McCormick Harvester and Twine Binder was a marvelous invention that not only harvested the crop, but would bind the wheat in twine ties. One is pictured here being used to harvest wheat on a farm southeast of Eddy in 1896. Wheat grows best in a dry, mild climate with the most successful method being dry farming. Wheat soon gave way to alfalfa, which flourished in the semi-tropical climate.

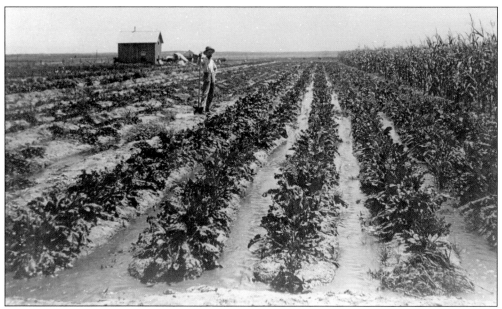

Experimental sugar beets attained great size in the soils of Eddy County. It was thought sugar beets were to be the crop of wealth for the Valley, but unfortunately those thoughts were to be short lived. Pest infestations were the principal cause of crop failure.

The Elberta variety of peach could reach a weight of up to one pound per fruit. R. M. Love sent a box of these peaches to Pres. Theodore Roosevelt from his Eddy orchard. Over 10,000 fruit trees were planted, lining the irrigation canals. In 1902, F. G. Tracy's 4.71 acres yielded $2,070.18 in peaches. Apples were a close second as an orchard favorite.

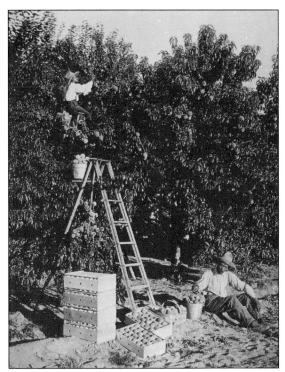

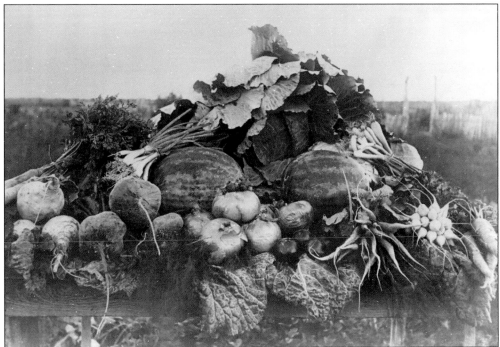

This photograph, among others, was used in promotional brochures to lure potential farmers into the Pecos Valley. Crops represented included sugar beets, watermelon, carrots, lettuce, potatoes, turnips, and onions. A bountiful harvest was promised in early brochures to all who settled and farmed in the area.

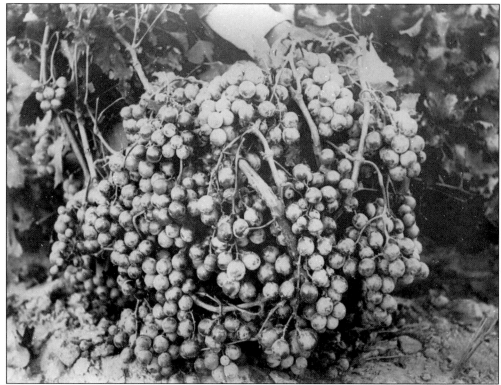

Shown is a prime sample of a grape cluster of the seedless Sultana variety raised by the Italian farmers who came to Eddy seeking better lives for themselves and their families. Descendants of several of the early Italian immigrant families, including the Cavanis, Grandis, and Fornis, are still in the Valley.

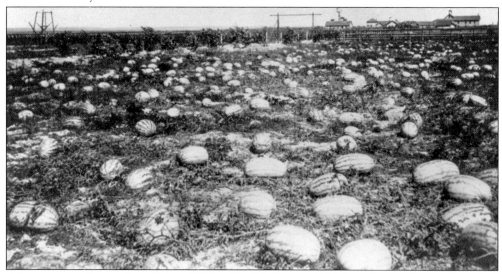

A large watermelon patch on Robert W. Tansill's Otis farm in 1895 shows how well crops flourished with irrigation. The sheer size and number of watermelons is a tribute to the sandy soil's ability to produce fruit. Shipping of such crops was made possible with the railroad built by J. J. Hagerman, but the lengthy route to markets caused heavy spoilage.

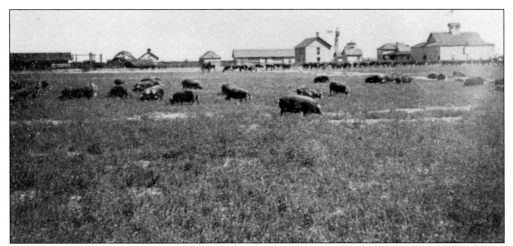

Robert Tansill's hog farm in Otis, a community south of Eddy, was a success with the hogs doing very well, fattened on alfalfa. Although cattle and horses were the main livestock in the valley, hogs were not subject to cholera here as in other parts of the country and raising hogs was expected to become an important industry in Eddy County.

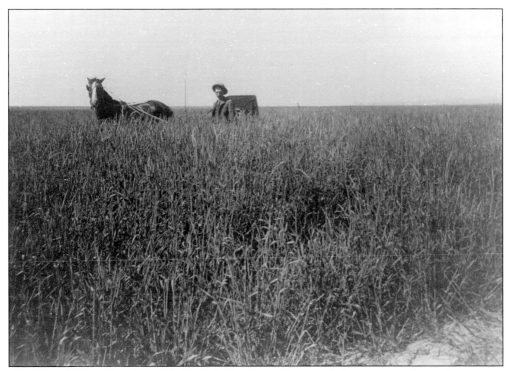

An 1896 photograph of a rye field on Bolles Farm illustrated the amount of growth possible. Richard Bolles bought 640 acres of land 5 miles south of Eddy to turn it into the finest racehorse ranch in this part of the country. Bolles built a racetrack west of Eddy and transported his superior racehorse stock from Colorado where he resided, using the Eddy farm during winter.

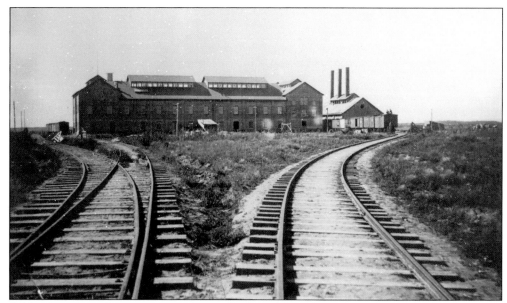

Schlitz Sugar Beet Factory processed sugar for the Schlitz Brewing Company in Carlsbad for only two seasons until it closed. The factory burned down in 1903, and the present-day newspaper, the *Current Argus*, is now situated on this location. Charles Eddy and Jeff Miller came up with the idea of selling sugar beet sugar to the breweries and J. J. Hagerman established the Pecos Valley Sugar Beet Company.

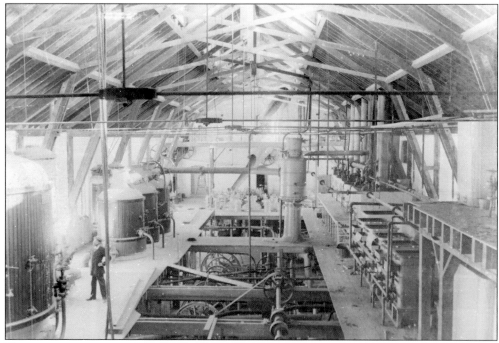

The interior operations of the Schlitz Sugar Beet Factory are pictured here. The quality and low sugar content of the sugar beet crop was disappointing. It was found that the sugar beets depleted the soil of nutrients too quickly, so when the factory burned down under mysterious circumstances, the industry was not revived.

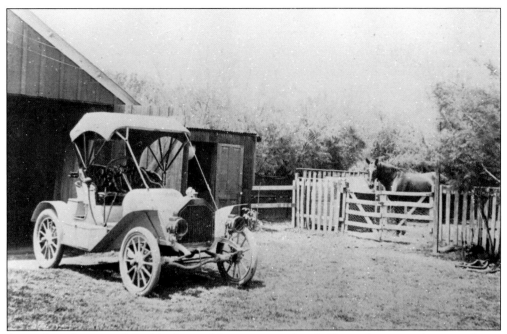

An early ordinance of Carlsbad stated "any person who shall race horses or drive any horse through the streets within the limits of town at a speed or gait to exceed 8 miles per hour shall be punished for such offense by a fine of not exceeding $25 or by imprisonment at the discretion of the court." This ordinance had to be revised later to include automobiles.

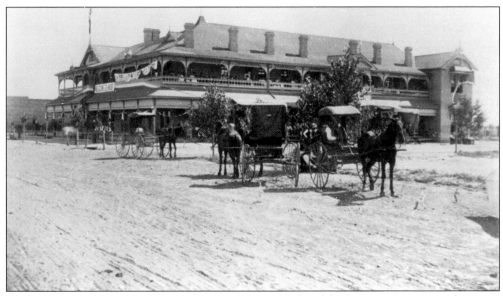

Pictured is the Schlitz Hotel in downtown Eddy. This hotel had many names over the years. Starting life as the Hagerman Hotel, it became the Schlitz Hotel, then the Windsor and finally the Bates Hotel before it burned in 1917. Upstairs provided shelter for critically ill patients of consumption for $40 per month, as there was no hospital until 1897.

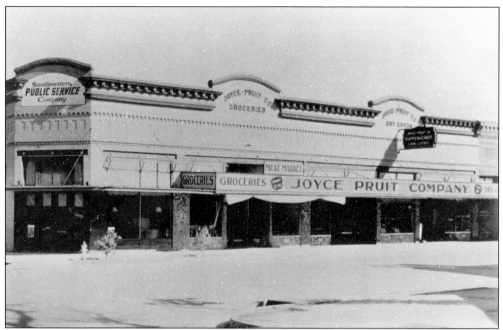

The Joyce Pruit Company Store, shown here in 1925, employed 50 people and was considered to be the largest mercantile in southeastern New Mexico. Its president, John Joyce, and vice president, Aurelius Pruit, branched out their business to include neighboring Roswell, providing that community as well with much-needed supplies. Members of the Joyce family still reside in Carlsbad.

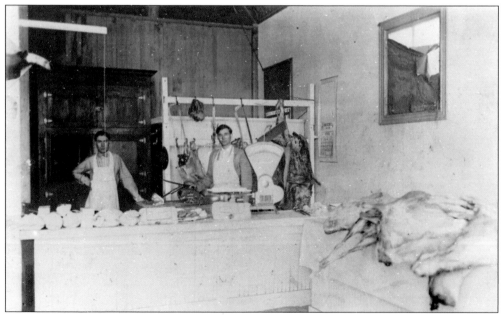

Fennessey and McLendon Meat Market was just one of the markets available to Eddy residents. Dave Kemp and his half-brother Walker Bush were also partners in a meat market in downtown Eddy in 1893. Dee Harkey began working in a meat market when he arrived in Eddy as a young man, before he was deputy sheriff. Meat was delivered in a two-wheeled cart drawn by a pony.

Five

IS THAT SMOKE?

Ancient people most likely knew about the large opening in the earth south of present-day Carlsbad, as is evidenced by rock art on the ledges above the natural entrance. When cowboy James Larkin White saw what he believed to be a trail of smoke from a volcano, he rode to investigate. The sight he witnessed puzzled him; it was not smoke, but millions of bats spiraling out of a cave opening.

Initial exploration amazed White, who entered the cave with only a kerosene lamp and a knife. When the lamp went out on one excursion, White was thrown into a complete inky darkness and silence, which rattled him for a few moments. Known for his determination, he explored his new discovery, telling people about his wonderful finds, only to have his enthusiasm met with indifference.

The cave drew the attention of the federal government in 1923 through the United States Department of Interior inspector Robert Holley, who was awestruck at the beauty he saw. Dr. Willis T. Lee, a geologist who visited the cave with his daughter Ann, wrote about it in his February 1924 article for *National Geographic*. Black and white photographs taken by Ray V. Davis were featured in a 1923 *New York Times* article, rousing wide interest as well. After federal and national recognition, the cave was recommended as a national monument.

Dr. Lee dreamed of cutting a tunnel through the mountain from the south end of the cave to provide easier access, calling it "Lee's Tunnel". The tunnel never came to fruition, much to Jim White's relief.

Carlsbad Caverns has seen millions of visitors pass through its doors since it was declared a national park in 1930. The underground beauty is still breathtaking, inspiring much the same reaction from many of the tourists today as Jim White experienced when he first stepped into the inky void in 1901.

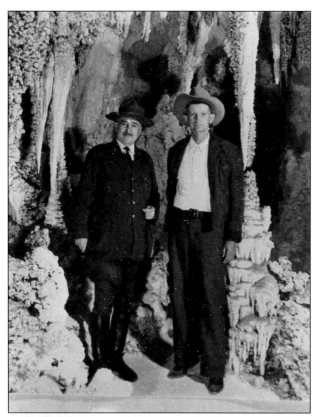

Local photographer Ray V. Davis captured this image of first superintendent Tom Boles, left, and Jim White, right, in 1928 in the Bat Cave. The location, Davis's favorite, became known as the Chinese Theater. Jim White, who is credited with discovering and promoting the cave, later became chief guide. Tom Boles was called "Mr. Carlsbad Caverns" by the local newspapers for his promotion of the cave.

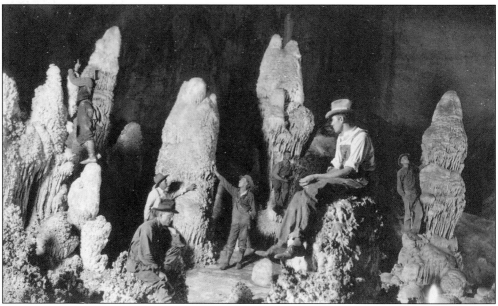

This early image of local residents posing against and on stalagmite formations in the Bat Cave is thought to be one of Ray V. Davis's most recognizable photos. It was not known at that time that stalagmites were formed by drops of mineral-laden water and would stop growing when coated with oils from the skin.

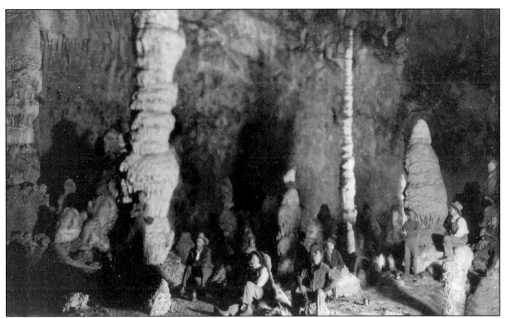

Early cave explorers were treated to beautiful sights of the white, pristine formations, which glistened like crystals under the photographer's lights. Jim White, wearing the large Stetson, is portrayed in this Ray V. Davis photograph surrounded by several guano mine workers. The picture was taken in the Bat Cave at the Totem Poles City of the Gods, a favorite photographic area.

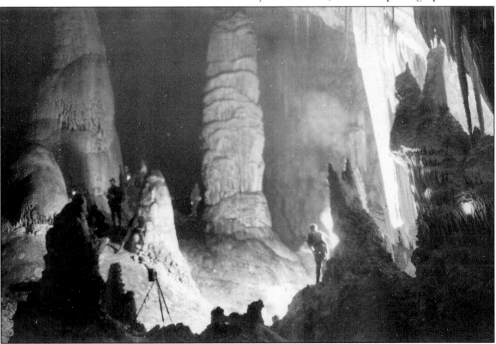

Stalagmites are formed from tiny drops of water filtering through the cracks. The massive flowstone stalagmites are smooth, while the smaller ones are a coralline or rougher surface. Both are formed by dissolved lime carbonate slowly dripped from the ceiling. These formations, given Native American and Greek mythological names in the beginning, continue to amaze visitors.

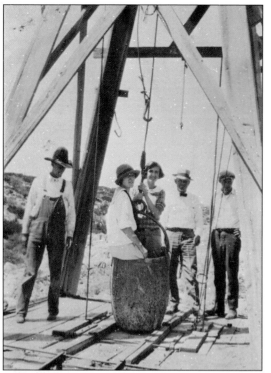

In 1924, explorers descended into the Bat Cave by riding down a metal bat guano bucket. Jim White's wife Fannie would scrub the iron buckets in order for them to have a less offensive odor to the explorers. Shown here from left to right are Adele Bujac and Mollie Culpepper, who followed Ann Lee, the first known woman to set foot in the Bat Cave.

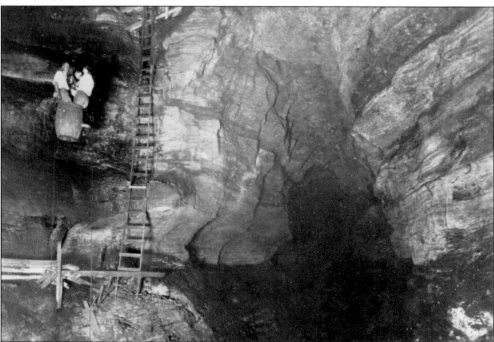

In 1924, a choice of descent by either guano bucket or ladder was given; most people chose the guano bucket. Once in the Bat Cave, the mile-and-a-half tour was given by Jim White personally. The Carlsbad Caverns still have some of the original ladders hanging on display in the cave to illustrate early cave exploration.

Once the Carlsbad Caverns became a national park, the guano bucket as a means of descent could no longer be used for the general public due to the high numbers of visitors anticipated. A wooden 216-step stairway named Jim White's Stairway was built in 1925. An elevator shaft was constructed in 1931 to allow even more people to enjoy the wonders.

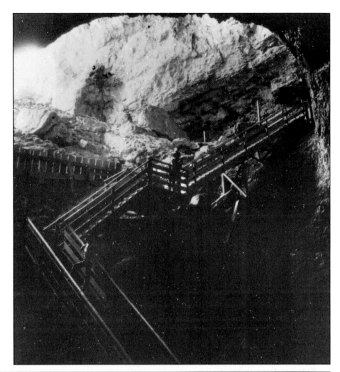

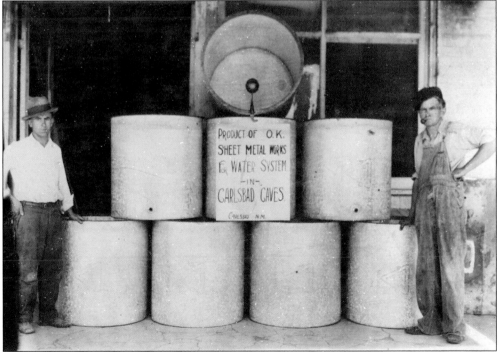

O.K. Blacksmith Company, owned by Ohnemus and Kircher, was one of Carlsbad's best-known early blacksmith shops, providing many blacksmithing and metal services for the Pecos Valley. Fabricated metal tubs used for the water system in the Carlsbad Caverns are shown in this 1925 photograph.

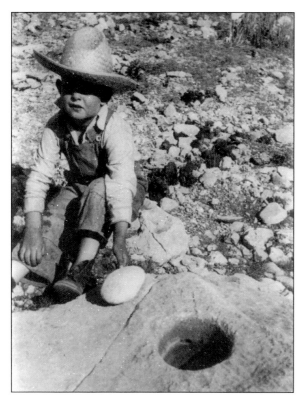

Young Jim White Jr. is pictured here with grinding holes carved into the limestone by local Native American tribes, who used them for milling seeds. Basket Makers, Comanche, and Mescalero Apache tribes roamed the area surrounding the Carlsbad Caverns. It is said the Native Americans were not big cave explorers, but one skeleton believed to be Native American was found within the cave.

Ray V. Davis's photograph "Giant Pillars of Stalagmites, Bat Cave" includes Jim White standing in the center wearing his trademark hat. Stalagmites are cave formations that have been formed on the ground from tiny drips of water generated from small cracks in the ceiling. The drips slide down the stalactite formations on the ceiling and create formations on the ground. After many years, the stalagmites might eventually reach the ceiling.

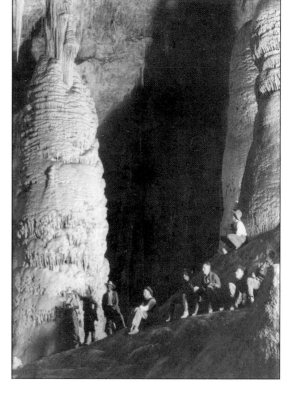

Elizabeth Garrett, the blind daughter of sheriff Patrick Garrett, visited the Carlsbad Caverns with her guide dog, Tenna. Garrett is best known for writing the New Mexico state song "Oh Fair New Mexico." She lived in Roswell for most of her life and is quoted as saying, "Quite frequently my father had to bring harmony with a gun. I always tried to do so by carrying a tune."

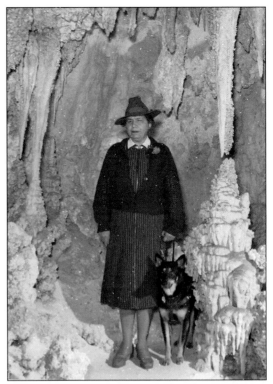

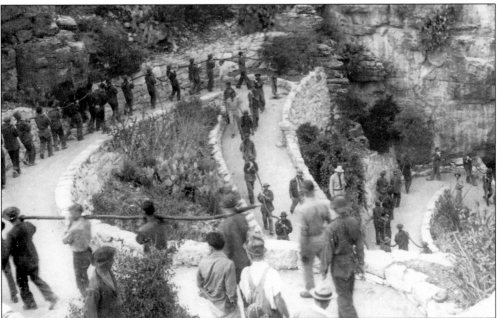

Pres. Franklin D. Roosevelt proposed a new program, the Civil Conservation Corps, intended to relieve the high unemployment rate of the Great Depression by putting men to work building roads, buildings, and schools. Civil Conservation Corps (CCC) workers are pictured here taking a main cable into the Carlsbad Caverns on the trails they built. The CCC built rock buildings used as housing at the Carlsbad Caverns, as well as walls at the Carlsbad beach.

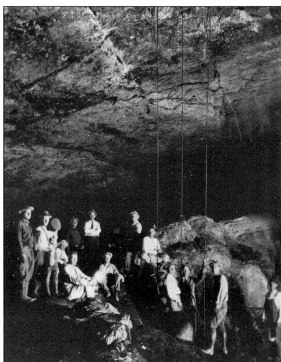

In 1924, an ascent in a guano bucket took visitors 170 feet up out of the cave using a wire rope fastened to an engine pulley at the top of a wooden derrick. The system caused concern for the weary visitors. Jim White would say, "The engine does not fail very often! But if it does, I can apply the friction brake before you drop very far!"

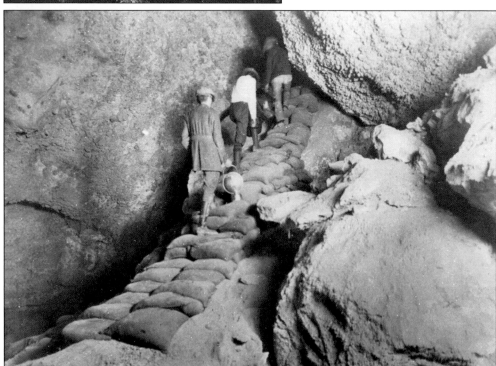

The Golden Staircase, as it was jokingly referred to by Jim White, used bags of bat guano to form trails for these 1924 visitors. The bags made the footing easier, as the damp cave floor could be quite slippery in spots. Dr. Willis Lee's daughter Ann is shown in the middle negotiating the trail.

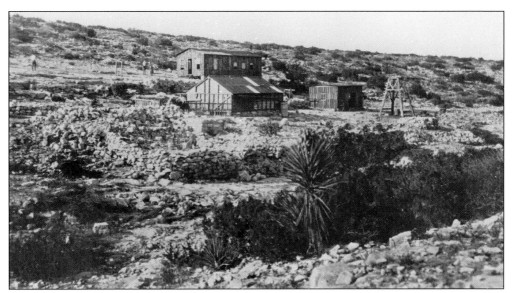

Pictured here is a guano mining operation set up near the natural entrance of the Bat Cave. The White family lived in a small house for several years as Jim tried to drum up support for the cave to be explored. Fannie White cooked dinner for the explorers and eventually, the Whites began charging $2 per person for a guided tour and food. The money was used to extend the trail deeper into the cave.

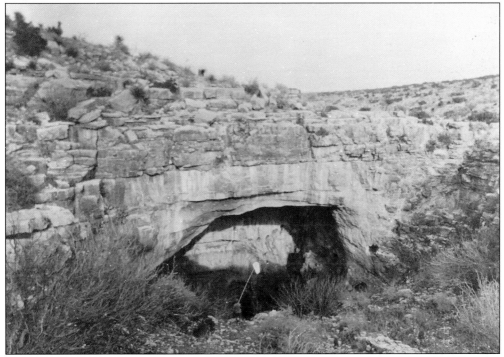

A man with butterfly net attempts to catch cave swallows. He was part of the 1924 National Geographic Society expedition led by Dr. Willis T. Lee. The swallows made a permanent colony at the Carlsbad Caverns entrance. Often mistaken for bats, the populations have risen to nearly 4,000 and have entertained park visitors with their aerial acrobatics over the years.

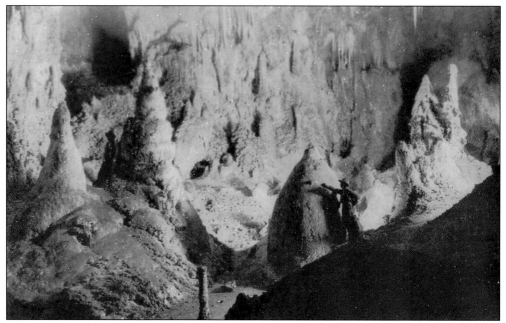

A 1926 Ray V. Davis photograph of Doh's Kiva in the Big Room of the Carlsbad Cave is shown here. Davis only asked a small cut for the distribution rights of any photograph taken by him in the cave. Davis was the first of many photographers to capture the beauty of the Carlsbad Caverns; Ennis Creed "Tex" Helm and the renowned Ansel Adams would follow in his footsteps.

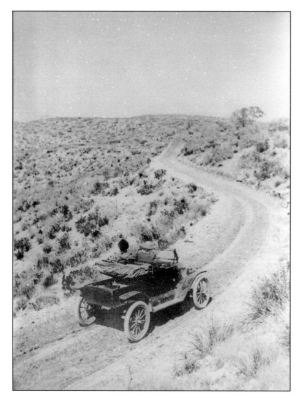

A couple is pictured on the first road to the Bat Cave in 1923 carved into the countryside by heavy road machinery. The meandering road rose steeply, making for dangerous travel in the early days. Although the road is paved today, it is still steep and winding. There are nature trails and informational stops along the 7-mile road to give visitors a tutorial on the desert setting.

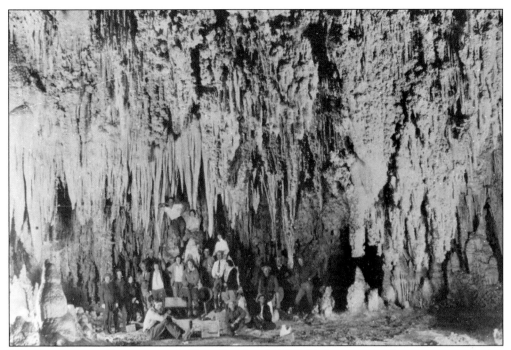

The first cavern radio party was held on October 4, 1922. Unfortunately, there was no reception in the cave. Frank Ernest Nicholson led a 15-man expedition to Carlsbad Caverns to test a radio experiment conceived by Eric Palmer to gauge penetration of the earth's crust by radio waves. The expedition was declared a success on February 20, 1930.

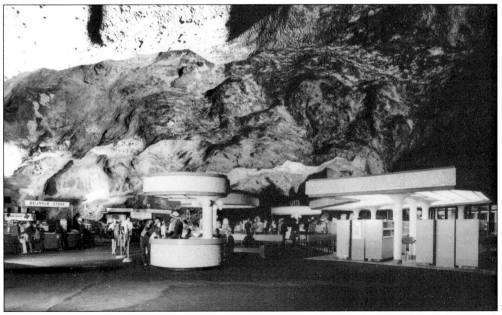

The Carlsbad Caverns' Lunch Room, pictured in this 1977 photograph, is 750 feet underground. The cave maintains a constant 56-degree temperature, which makes for a pleasant tour. Visitors are able to purchase and eat a boxed lunch, usually consisting of a sandwich and potato chips. Carlsbad Caverns curios are also for sale in the lunchroom.

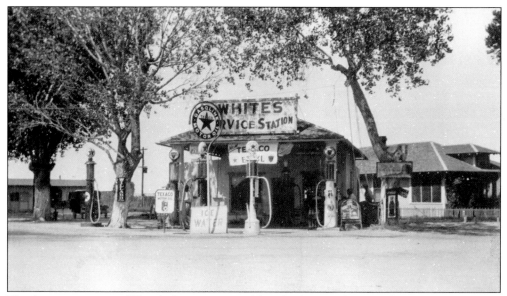

The first gas station in White's City was opened by Charles L. White. Without having seen the cave, he filed homestead papers for the land at the mouth of Walnut Canyon in order to capitalize on the Carlsbad Cavern phenomenon. White's City now consists of several hotels, a grocery store, café, gas station, and souvenir shop. White and his family, who were not related to Jim White, have since disposed of the property.

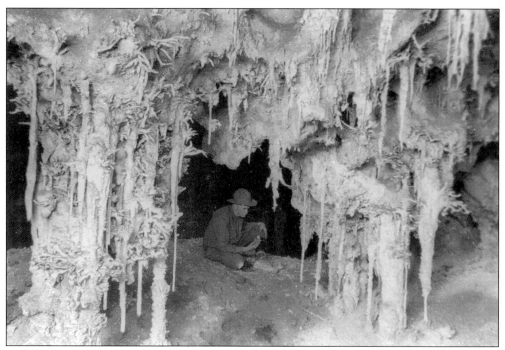

Dr. Willis T. Lee, a Pennsylvanian geologist for the National Geographic Society, is pictured studying pieces of stalactites while sitting amongst a soda-straw formation. Dr. Lee was fascinated with the Carlsbad Caverns and returned many times with his daughter Ann to visit the magnificence that lay beneath the desert surface.

Six

FROM POTASH TO THE NUCLEAR AGE

While looking for oil in 1925, Dr. V. H. McNutt, geologist for Snowden and McSweeney Oil Company, discovered the largest potash deposit in the United States by finding salt crystals in a 1,000-foot core sample drilled east of Carlsbad. Potash is a chemical combination of the element potassium with one or more other elements. In this case, the potash was potassium chloride oxide, commonly called K20. Typically used for fertilizer, potash was also utilized in explosives, glass making, and glass for optical lenses.

Potash ore is laid down in solid beds with no structural faults or intruding boulders. Typical underground rooms in a potash mine had 14-foot ceilings and were 40 feet wide without support timbers; roof bolts were used instead. Mine production began in earnest in 1930, with U.S. Borax opening the first mine.

The Atomic Energy Commission established Plowshare projects to provide research and development directed toward peaceful uses of nuclear explosives. The first nuclear test of these projects, and the most advanced, was Project Gnome. The project tested many scientific objectives, and called for the detonation of a 5-kiloton nuclear device about 1,200 feet underground at the end of a 1,116 foot hooked tunnel that was supposed to self-seal upon detonation. A column of radioactive smoke and steam rose from the tunnel after the December 11, 1961, blast. The experiment was not considered to be successful.

As the use of radiation and related products rose, the need for nuclear storage became paramount. Amidst many years of opposition, the Waste Isolation Pilot Plant (WIPP) was built to house low-level nuclear waste consisting of contaminated gloves, medical waste, industrial tissue, and the like in the salt beds southeast of Carlsbad. A mile-and-a-half deep shaft was sunk into the salt, and rooms formed much like the potash mines to house the waste with the idea that eventually the rooms will self implode, sealing the waste in the salt. Special containers called TRUPACTs are used to haul the waste to the WIPP site on the backs of satellite-tracked semi-trucks.

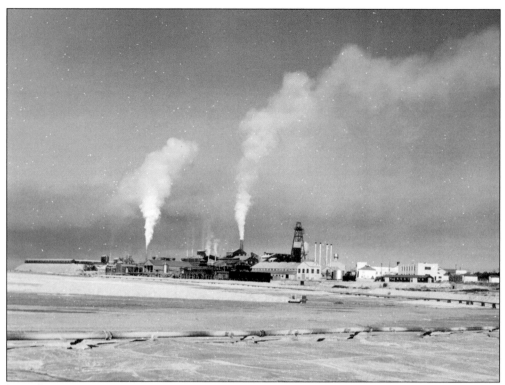

Steam rises from Potash Company of America's processing smoke stacks. Although mostly steam, the vapor is mixed with tiny amounts of potash, which settles on the land and objects around the plant. This 1950 picture also shows the salt lake surrounding the mine operations, which forms a hard surface over time caused by the clay, salt, and brine contents of the water.

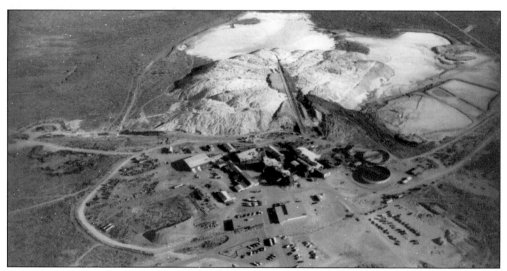

A 1977 aerial shot shows the Mississippi Chemical potash mine. Since its discovery, the potash mining industry has been a major source of income for Carlsbad and surrounding areas. By the mid-1960s, there were six mines operating in the Permian Basin. Today only two survive, but continue to be large producers in the potash market.

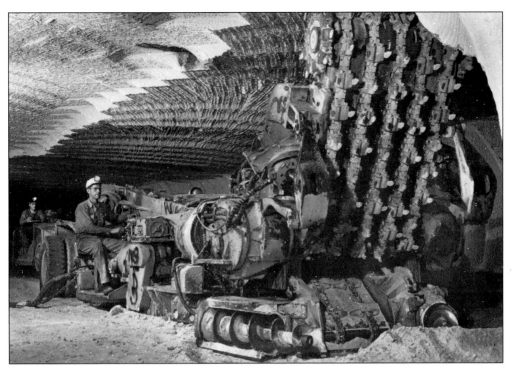

In 1955, Potash Company of America used tungsten drill bits on rotating steel drums to scrape the potash ore from the mine face and pull ore from the walls, thus creating the labyrinths. Shown is what was known as a "Ripper Miner." Designed and used exclusively by Potash Company of America, the miner had a conveyor belt connected directly to it so shuttle cars were not necessary.

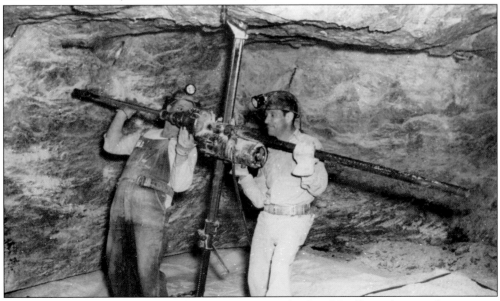

This piece of equipment is called a Twin Boom Jumbo Roof Driller, otherwise known as a "mankiller" by the men who used it. The driller weighed over 100 pounds and was difficult to control while trying to drill dynamite holes into the wall of the mine, since it required two men to raise and lower it by hand.

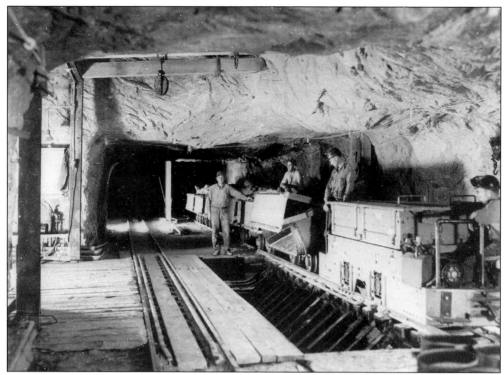

United States Potash Company was one of the first mines in the Permian Basin. Granby-type car bins were used in 1946 to haul potash ore through the mine to the processing area, dumping the ore on a conveyor belt. This photograph was labeled as being taken at the foot of shaft No. 1.

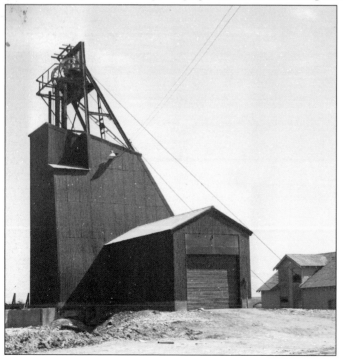

The tall building to the left is the hoist over shaft No. 1 at the Potash Company of America site, which brings the potash ore carts or skips out of the mine by means of levers and a pulley system. A mine employee would sit in the hoist house shown to the right of the shaft, lifting ore cars out manually to begin the surface processing.

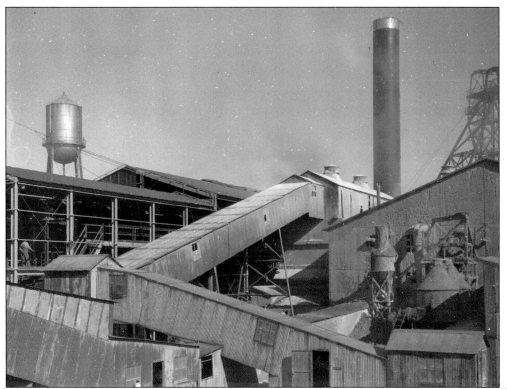

The conveyor belt system used to hoist refined potash ore to the warehouses is in the housing shown. This 1946 photograph of the Potash Company of America's conveyor belt housing system was taken from the top of a 75-foot tank situated across from the main processing plant.

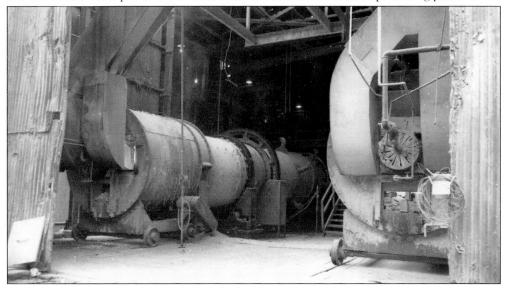

Wet processed potash is placed inside dryers to remove the water and solutions used to remove soil and clay from the ore. The dryer temperatures reach 350 degrees due to the 10- to 15-foot flame inside the cylinders. The ridges around the outside contain knockers, which agitate the ore inside the dryers, breaking it up.

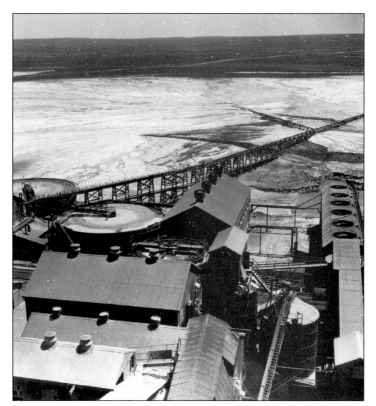

This photograph taken from the top of the hoist shows the mining operations of the Potash Company of America in 1946. The mine is a closed circuit system until it gets to the end at the Rougher Cells, which consist of huge screens submerged in water and other solutions. Once the ore is cleaned, screened, and processed it is loaded into rail cars for shipment.

A potash ore train at the Potash Company of America is shown here. Hall Machine of Carlsbad designed and built the first rail cars to haul ore to market. In 1952, the 100,000th railcar load of refined product was shipped from the International Minerals and Chemicals Corporation mine. The restored engine from the first potash train is located at the municipal beach area.

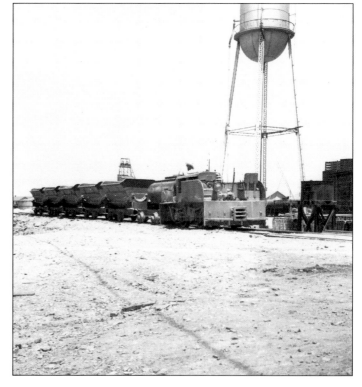

The safety float representing Potash Company of America in the 1946 Labor Day parade illustrates cause and effect, since safety is always a major concern for any mining operation. Unfortunately, as with any mining operation, there have been several mine deaths over the years. Safety is of the utmost importance to the mine operations and to the community that supplies the workers. Carlsbad's Mine Rescue Team has won many awards.

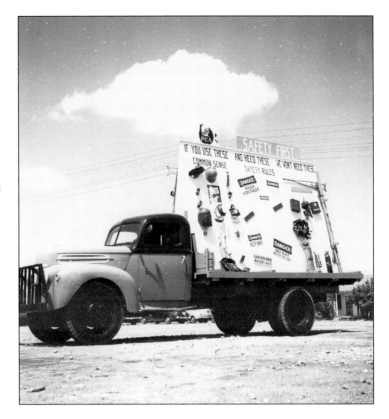

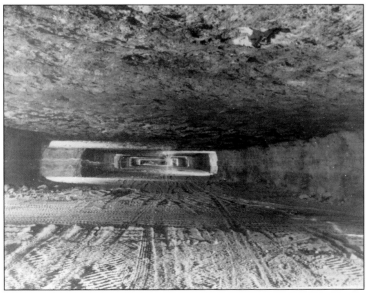

This view looks down what is called the drift in the Mississippi Chemical Potash Mine in 1977. Any horizontal or sub-horizontal development opening is given the generic name of "the drift." These openings are cut from the ore face by a piece of machinery called the Miner. There are several thousand miles of mining drifts under the surface southeast of Carlsbad.

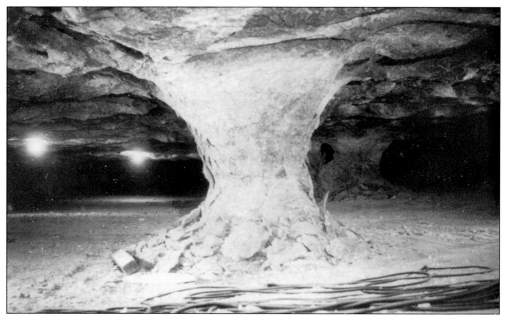

This salt pillar was left from excavation of the drift by a miner. The potash mines of southern New Mexico employ the room and pillar mining system, one of the oldest known mining methods. In this system, ore is removed across a horizontal plane, leaving pillars of ore to support the overburden caused by leaving open room underground. Pillars must be large enough to support, preventing a collapse.

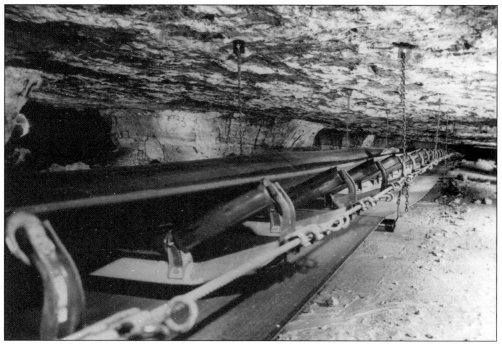

Pictured here is the underground steel cord conveyor belt that brought the unrefined ore to the shuttle cars, which would then be hoisted to the surface for refining. The conveyor belt is a continuous belt wound around two drums that drop ore into waiting carts.

Oil and gas have provided the Pecos Valley with one of its largest employment industries. The first oil well was drilled in Carlsbad in 1908. Drilling began in earnest around Carlsbad in the 1920s, but did not take off until the late 1950s. The industry has seen many ups and downs over the years, having an impact on the economy of Carlsbad and the surrounding area.

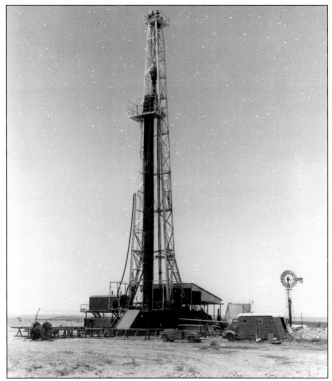

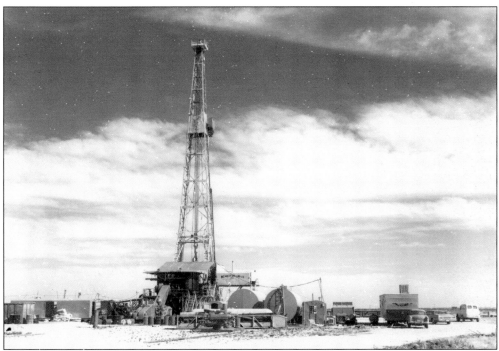

A Big West Drilling Company oil rig is shown in this 1972 photograph. Many oilmen during the 1970s and 1980s said that the only way for them to survive was to drill deep and operate the wells themselves. Deep wells at depths of 15,000 feet or more were not regulated at that time.

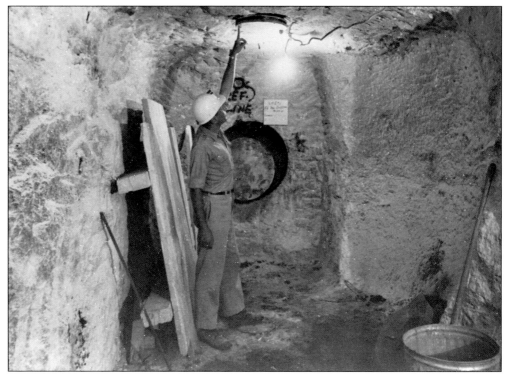

A man stands in the detonation chamber of Project Gnome in July 1961, five months before the actual detonation took place. It was expected the cavity would remain intact, with a spherical form 110 feet in diameter, with a pool at the bottom of about 6,000 tons of molten salt. The temperature of the molten salt was expected to be about 1,440 degrees Fahrenheit.

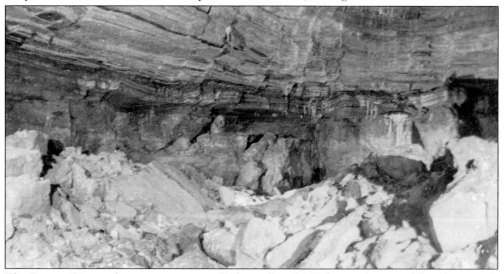

The Project Gnome detonation cavity is 80 feet tall and 200 feet in diameter. The photograph was taken one year after detonation, and the destruction is evident. Many dignitaries were invited to witness the historical event from the protection of several miles away from the actual bombsite. President Kennedy approved the project on October 25, 1961. A slab marker is now the only indication of the site.

80

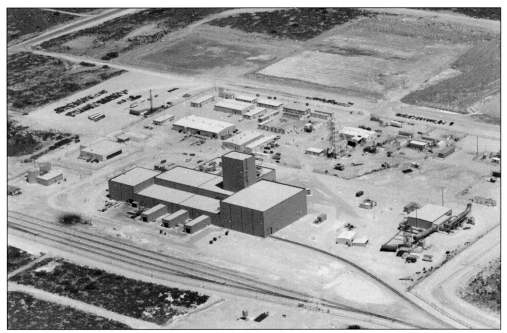

An aerial shot shows the Waste Isolation Pilot Plant, locally known as WIPP, in 1987. The plant has now grown to nearly double the size in the photograph. An extensive yearlong training program for employees ensures that the quality of waste handling and treatment meets and exceeds the already-stringent government standards.

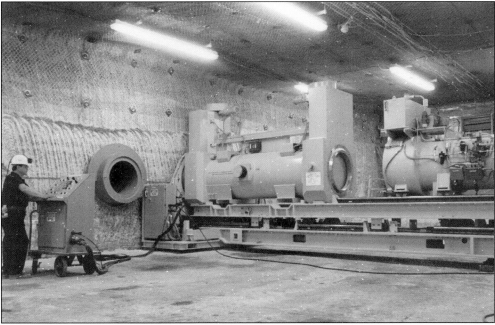

The storage of low-level nuclear waste has provided Carlsbad with a major employer in the Waste Isolation Pilot Plant. The facility is a vast network of corridors excavated out of the salt beds 1.5 miles below the surface. The machine shown inserts cylinders of waste into storage tubes drilled into the salt, which is thought to be the safest way to store the waste products.

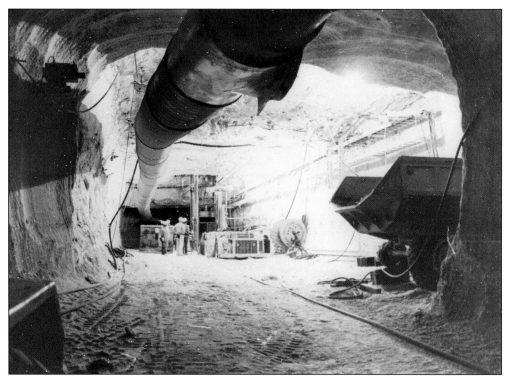

The Waste Isolation Pilot Plant received its first waste shipment in 2001 from the Savannah River Site. Extensive archives and libraries around the world store information that will inform and warn future generations of WIPP's existence. Heavy equipment and construction items were taken underground piece by piece

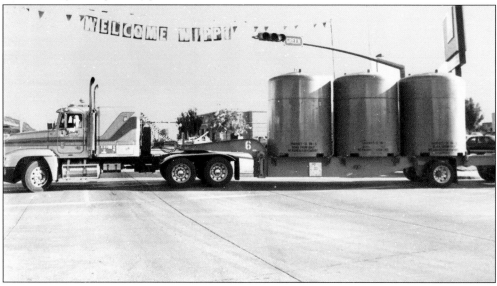

A satellite-tracked TRU-PACT truck is welcomed to downtown Carlsbad in 1991. After many years and a large amount of controversy, the Waste Isolation Pilot Plant opened, bringing low-level nuclear waste to be stored in the salt beds. TRU-PACTs have been rigorously tested and contain specially manufactured seals and gaskets, which have never leaked.

Seven

SOME GAVE ALL

Carlsbad has had a long, proud, and distinctive military history, beginning with many of its residents serving as soldiers on both sides of the Civil War, and continuing on to present-day soldiers fighting in the wars in Iraq and Afghanistan. The call to service is always heard loud and strong by the men and women of Carlsbad.

The National Guard was established in 1909 under the command of Etienne P. Bujac. It saw service not only in New Mexico protecting the Mexican border, but was immediately sent to France in World War I with the 40th Brigade. Back home in 1919, the veterans formed the Carlsbad American Legion, naming it in honor of their only casualty, Bryan Mudgett.

Among the 1,800 members of the 200th and 515th Coastal Artillery who were taken captive in Bataan, the Philippines, only 900 returned home. Of those, only 600 survived the first year of peacetime. Of the 12,000 men who were forced on the Bataan Death March, one in six was from New Mexico. Many of the casualties occurred on the "Hell Ships," so called because of the horrible conditions used by the Japanese to transport prisoners to Japan or Manchuria. American submarines unknowingly and tragically torpedoed several of these ships. Both of local photographer Ray V. Davis's sons, Dewayne and Eugene, fell victim to the sinking of the "Hell Ship" *Arisan Maru*.

Every military action took its toll on Carlsbad in the form of casualties and missing in action soldiers. The Vietnam War resulted in the MIA/POW Memorial being erected at the Carlsbad beach area; 12 trees were planted to represent each soldier remembered.

No matter which war or conflict fought, the soldiers of Carlsbad and their families showed valor and bravery. Whether serving in the armed forces during war or peacetime, or paying the ultimate sacrifice, a humbled Carlsbad bids a heartfelt thank-you. Their efforts will not go forgotten.

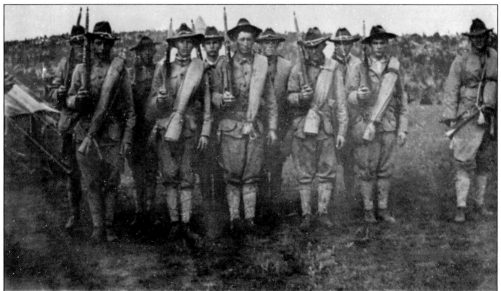

Company B, 1st Militia of New Mexico, pictured here in 1898, participated in the Mexican Punitive Expedition. Maj. Gen. John J. Pershing led the expedition after the March 16, 1916, attack on Columbus, New Mexico, by Mexican outlaw Francisco "Pancho" Villa and nearly 500 of his revolutionists. This expedition was called one of America's "little wars" and served as a training ground and prelude to World War I.

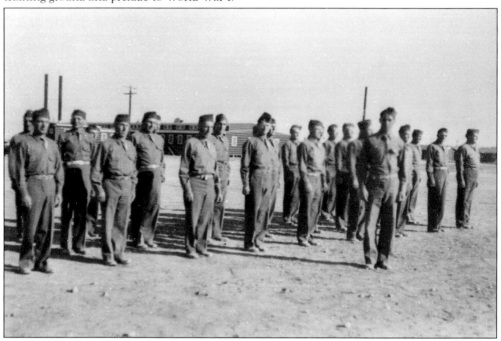

An unidentified unit is pictured in 1942 at the Carlsbad Army Air Field located 5 miles south of Carlsbad at the airport. The base was used to train bombardiers and navigators for World War II as the first and only low-altitude D-8-type bombardier school in the country. The base was closed immediately after the end of the war in 1945. The Carlsbad Municipal Airport is now located on the site.

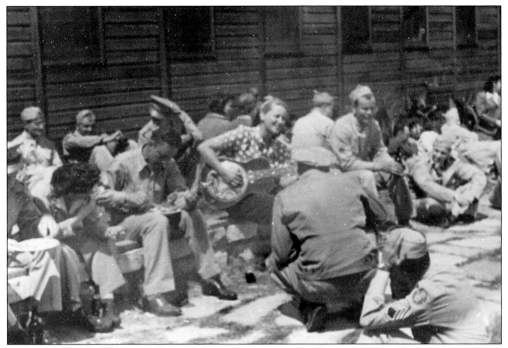

This 1943 photograph was taken at a barbeque held at the closed Civilian Conservation Corps Camp at Rattlesnakes Springs. During World War II, the camp was taken over by the Carlsbad Army Air Field. Events such as these, sponsored by the United Service Organizations, were commonplace at the base as well.

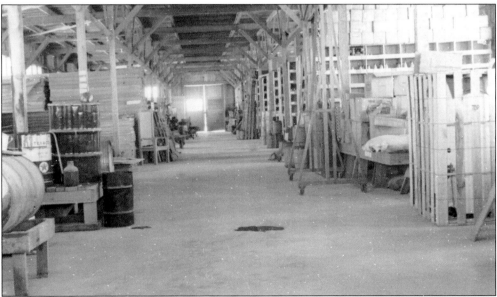

A supply warehouse located at the Carlsbad Army Air Field is pictured here in 1943. The army base was a city within itself, boasting a library, telephone exchange, post office, post exchange, gymnasium, enlisted men's service club, hospital, church, headquarter buildings, a residential district of barracks, theater, officer's club, non-commissioned officers club, control tower, weather station, commissary, radio station, fire department, and a separate civilian housing area.

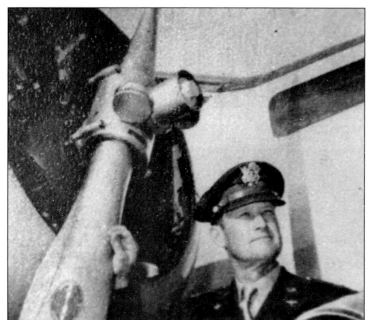

Col. William C. Lewis, commander of the Carlsbad Army Air Field, took charge on July 13, 1942, the day the field was activated. The airfield was a tract of 1,634 acres 5 miles south of Carlsbad, originally purchased by the city for use as an airport. Since construction had just begun on housing, temporary headquarters were set up in the Civilian Conservation Corps camp 3 miles north of Carlsbad.

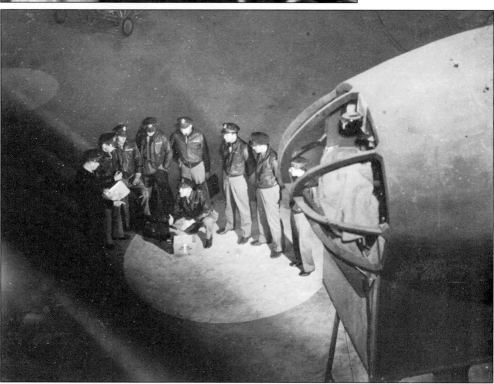

A meeting of some of the students at the Carlsbad Army Air Field is shown in this 1944 photograph. The students met concerning the top secret Norden Bombsight, which would be housed at only a few airfields, including Carlsbad. The Norden Bombsight was used by the United States during World War II to aid bombardiers to pinpoint their targets more precisely. It was brought to the Carlsbad Army Air Field under complete secrecy and heavy guard.

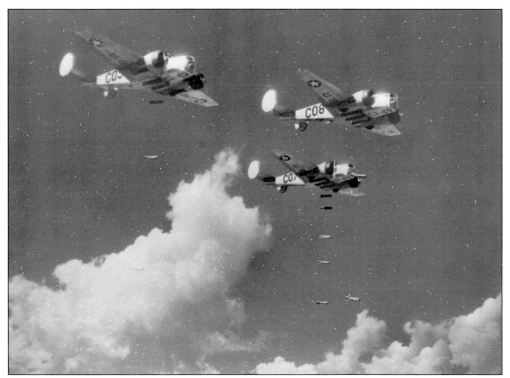

The Carlsbad Army Air Field hosted training for bombardiers from around the United States as well as two classes from China. There are approximately 26 military geoglyph bombing ranges around the Carlsbad area, some featuring swastikas, factories, ships, and bull's-eyes that can be plainly seen from the air, but look like dirt mounds on the ground. Each aircraft carried ten practice bombs that weighed 100 pounds each.

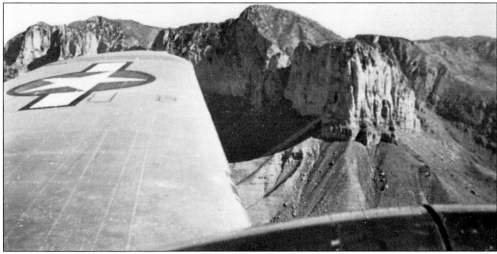

A unique perspective of Signal Peak, otherwise known as El Capitan, Texas, southwest of Carlsbad as seen from the cockpit of a Beechcraft AT-11 in 1942. The twin-engine, glass-nosed AT-11 was used by 90 percent of all trainees in the United States. Although there were 1,584 AT-11s made during World War II, the airplane is rare today. The first airplane assigned to the field was the BT-13A Valiant Trainer.

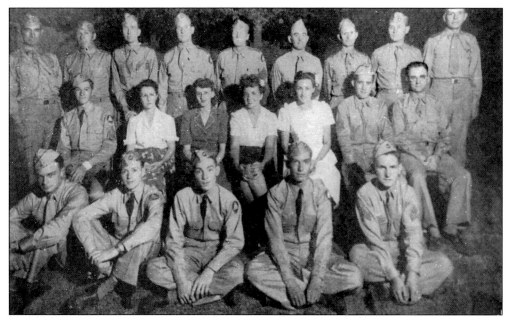

Carlsbad Civil Air Patrol is shown in this 1943 photograph taken at the Carlsbad Army Air Field. The Civil Air Patrol was organized in time of national crisis, mobilizing citizens to defend their country at a moment's notice, which earned them the name "The Flying Minutemen."

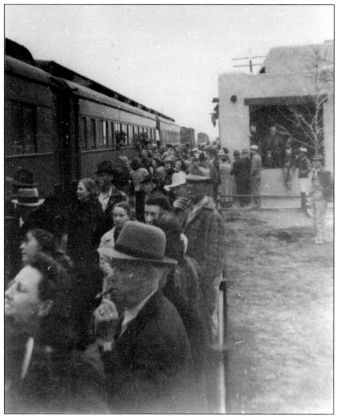

A crowd of Carlsbad citizens gathers at the Carlsbad Railroad Depot to give local members of the 200th and 515th Coast Artillery National Guard Unit a rousing sendoff. Called "The Regiment," they were known to be one of the best anti-aircraft units and were among the first to bring down a Japanese aircraft. Little did anyone know the horrors that would befall them after they landed in the Philippines.

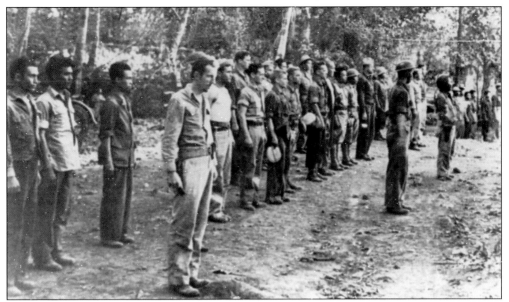

American prisoners of war are shown in formation in this 1942 photograph of Bataan, the Philippines. Several of Carlsbad's own are among these men. Among those pictured in this photograph are local men Joe Stanley Smith, Paul Womack, and Dick Malone. Dewayne Davis and Floyd Ward, also shown, were casualties of the POW camps.

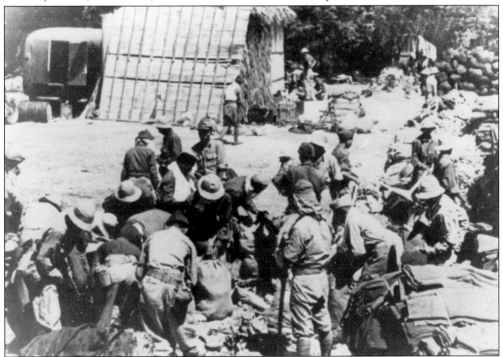

American soldiers were stripped of their duffle bags and keepsakes after being forced to surrender to Japanese forces after the three-month-long Battle of Bataan in 1942. The American soldiers were required to remain on the right side of the marching line and the Filipino soldiers were on the left; any deviation would result in a beating or worse.

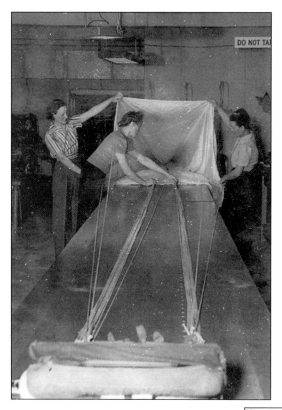

Mary Montgomery, far left, and two unidentified women are shown folding parachutes at the Carlsbad Army Air Field in 1943. Parachute folding requires a high degree of skill, as an improperly folded parachute will not open. No talking was allowed in the packing shed to assure full attention to the task. The canopies were typically made of silk until the supply was no longer available due to the Pacific War, and were then made from rayon.

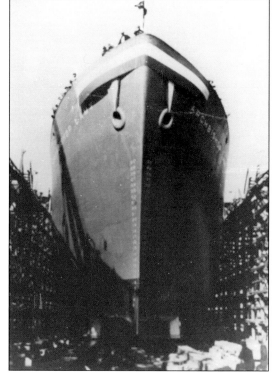

The Liberty ship *Archbishop Lamy* is an example of the 2,710 cargo ships hurriedly built between 1941 and 1945 to fill the need of the armed forces during World War II. Many women were employed in the shipyards to replace the men who were deployed. Any group that could raise war bonds worth $2 million could choose a name for a Liberty ship.

Eight

PEOPLE, PLACES, AND EVENTS

A cast of characters made up the people of the Pecos Valley. Unfortunately, there is not room to tell each of these stories, whether it be tragic or highly successful, or somewhere in between, although each is unique and worth the time. Added in this book are only a scant few of the people and events that shaped Carlsbad into what it is today. Being civil servants or businessmen, they are all adventurers, who molded the community, facing the good and bad with bravado and true grit.

Celebrations were frequent. A holiday, a rodeo, or the pecan were all reasons to throw a parade, have a festival, or crown a queen, and these events were looked forward to by people of every age. People would line the parade routes and children eagerly awaited a piece of candy thrown from the fire trucks. The parades would travel northward up Canal Street to Church Street and turn the corner to travel south on Canyon Street. Over the years, the original parade route was altered to go north on Canyon Street and end at the beach parking lot in order not to tie up traffic on the major roadway going through town.

The rodeos always drew a huge crowd dressed in boots and cowboy hats. Rodeos at all levels from junior to professional thrilled all onlookers. The rodeos, originally held on the high school football field, produced many champions from Carlsbad and Eddy County. A favorite event at early rodeos was called tournament and resembled jousting, as mounted riders raced down lines with spears in their hands to see who could spear the most hanging rings. This practice has been discontinued through the years.

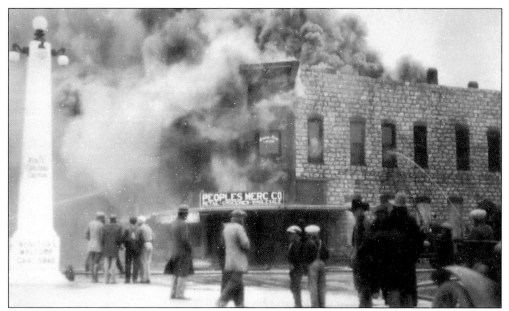

A fire erupted on the corner of Fox and Canyon Streets at the People's Mercantile in downtown Carlsbad. Short hoses made it difficult to reach a fire on the top level of buildings, so bucket brigades were used. In one incident, a fireman dropped a bucket off the roof onto the head of another fireman, who sued him for maliciously dropping the bucket. The first fireman was fined $1.

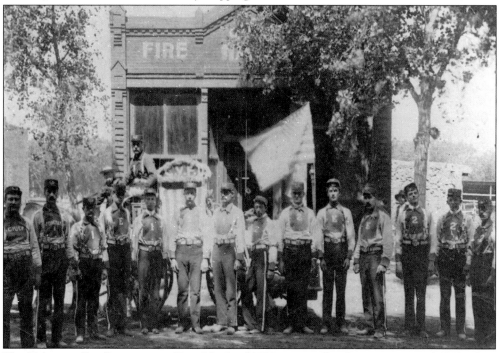

The Volunteer Fire Department, Hose No. 2, of 1893 was an all-volunteer unit until 1919, when the fire department was formed and the men were paid $1 per fire. A brand new $1,200 Babcock Chemical Engine was a welcome relief to the men, who were used to fighting fires using the hand-drawn water wagon and hose unit.

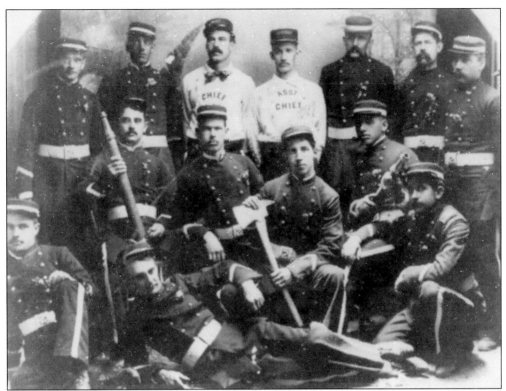

The fire department was manned by elite men, many of foreign birth. The firemen also formed the first band, which would play at the drop of a hat. Pictured here, from left to right, are the following members of the fire department: (first row) M. T. Kerr, Ed Piontowski, and C. Greene; (second row) I. H. Gilmore, A. R. Teeple, Sam Cook, and E. Balcomb; (third row) Bill Erwan, Ed Motter, E. D. Orr, Bill McLean, W. T. Reed, and P. Kircher.

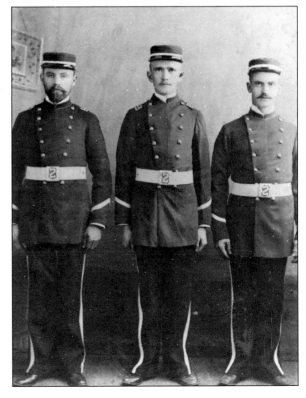

The original three members of Volunteer Fire Department, Hose No. 2, in 1893 were Alex Rogers (left), William McEwin (center), and A. Cole. The local newspaper, the *Eddy Argus*, described the volunteer fire department as "able, discreet, and partly sober." The fire department and city hall shared quarters at the corner of Canal Street and Fox Street for many years.

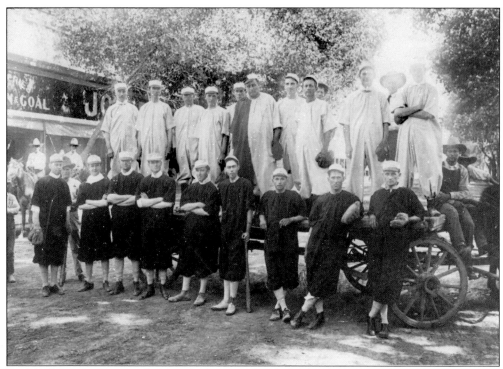

Carlsbad's baseball team exhibition had one pitcher for both sides; notice the pitcher's uniform is half black and half white. It is said there was a woman on the team as well, a rarity for 1911. The baseball team was first fielded in 1896, playing exciting games with neighboring communities, especially Roswell, as their fiercest competition. Fans would sometimes fill special train cars to attend the games.

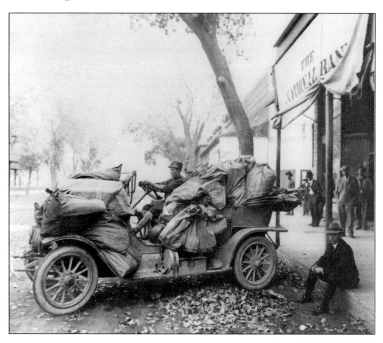

A 1910 German Kesel Touring car is parked in front of the Carlsbad Post Office with the front of the Bates Hotel visible in the background to the left. The car was used to deliver mail to the Eastern Plains of New Mexico. Standing in the right of the photograph with both hands in his pockets is Herman Hargis, and the driver is Shorty Ellis.

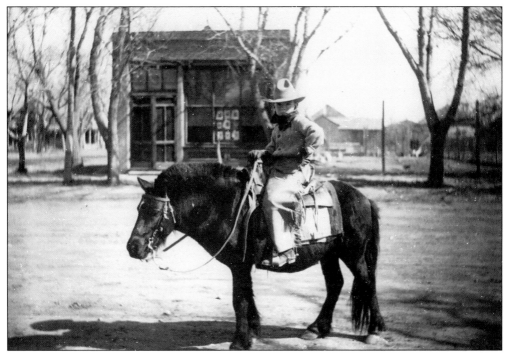

John R. Joyce is pictured on his favorite Shetland pony in front of Robb Photo Studio in 1910. Joyce became a large ranch owner and contributor to the local newspaper. He built a large estate on the East Hill at the edge of town across from the J. J. Hagerman estate, on Hagerman Heights.

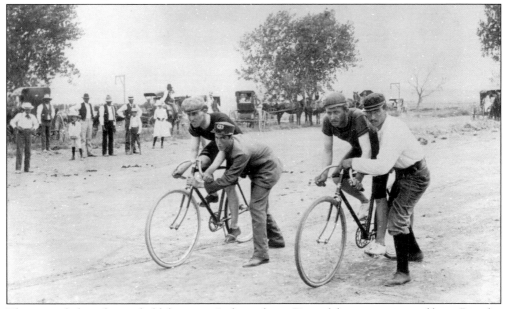

The start of a bicycle race held during an Independence Day celebration is pictured here. Bicycles were a favored mode of transportation—even sheriff Cicero Stewart and constable Dee Harkey used them to patrol the streets of Eddy. However, they soon found out a horse was a better means of apprehension when a man wanted for murder charged the pair with his horse, leaving the sheriff battered and bleeding on the streets of Phenix.

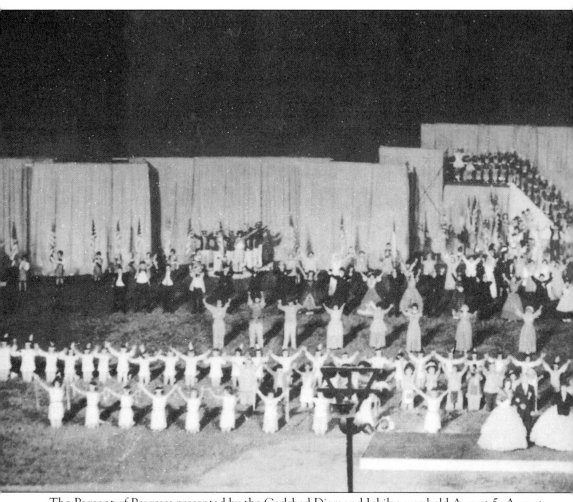

The Pageant of Progress presented by the Carlsbad Diamond Jubilee was held August 5–August 10, 1963, to celebrate the 75th anniversary of the founding of Carlsbad. A cast of hundreds brought history to life, and people wore period clothing. The winner of the Jubilee Queen contest, Francine Sims, was awarded a six day stay in Honolulu with a companion of her choice.

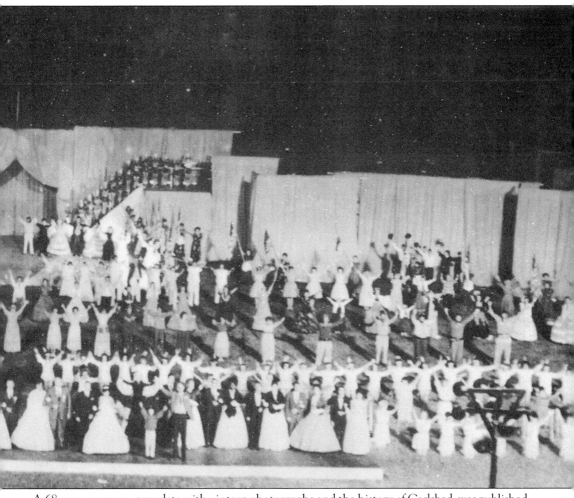

A 68-page program, complete with vintage photographs and the history of Carlsbad, was published to commemorate the event, and photograph exhibits were set up to educate the citizens of their long and proud heritage.

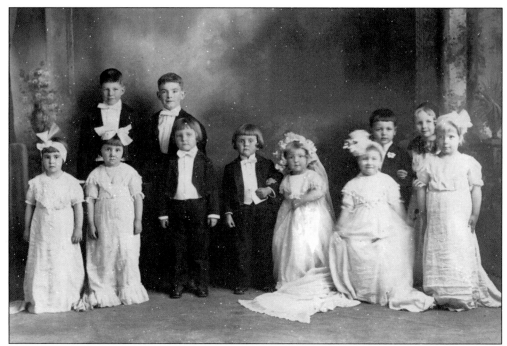

The cast of a Tom Thumb wedding, sponsored by the Woman's Club of Carlsbad in 1913, is pictured here. The miniature weddings became popular after world-famous dwarf and P. T. Barnum performer Charles "General Tom Thumb" Stratton married Lavinia Warren, another dwarf, in 1863. Churches and other organizations used the Tom Thumb weddings as a fund-raiser or children's activity. These weddings were hugely popular during the first half of the 20th century.

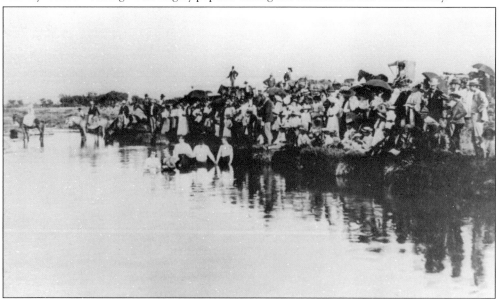

A mass baptism at Black River is featured in this 1893 photograph. Black River was a popular fishing spot and swimming hole for the citizens of Lookout, and later Loving. It continues to be a resort and religious retreat today. It was estimated that half of the population of Eddy is shown in this photograph.

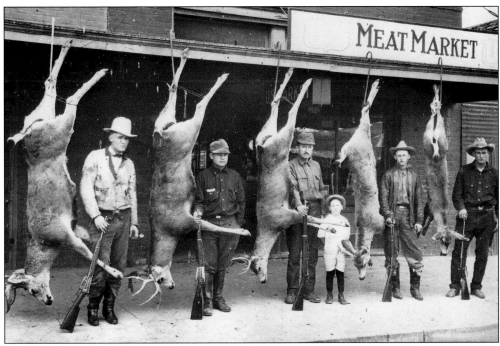

Deer hunters show off their quarry in 1925 in front of the meat market where the venison will be processed. These men used a lever action rifle to bring down their prey. Hunting was for both sport and survival, and mule deer were plentiful in the hills surrounding Carlsbad. A hunter could go out early in the morning and have his deer by 10:00 a.m.

In the long hot days of summer, many Carlsbad residents would spend their days at what is known to the locals as the Beach. The Beach is an area close to downtown Carlsbad and has evolved over the years. In 1924, a three-story diving tower was constructed, much to the delight of swimmers. Bathing suit rentals were available at the concession stand for those who did not own or bring a suit.

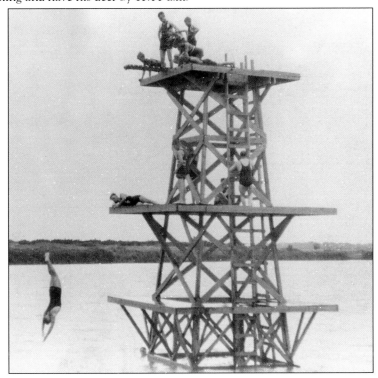

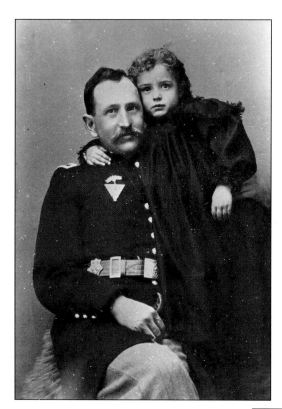

Dr. Anson A. Bearup, shown with four-year-old daughter Mabel, was Eddy's first dentist and was known for his keen sense of humor and dentistry skill. Dr. Bearup came to Eddy from the gold mining town of White Oaks in northern Lincoln County.

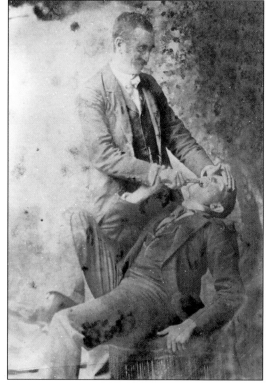

Dr. Anson A. Bearup is shown in this humorous photograph with a patient. He would play his phonograph loudly whenever drilling the tooth of a patient with his foot pedal drill. His office was located next to an outdoor theater. Whenever he had a late patient, the lights from his office would project everything the person was experiencing to the back of the screen.

Pictured in this 1895 Eddy studio photograph are *Eddy Argus* newspaper editor Mr. Goldberg (left), photographer J. F. Butler, and Dr. Anson Bearup, who is standing in the background with a stuffed bird. It was most likely taken with a camera timer.

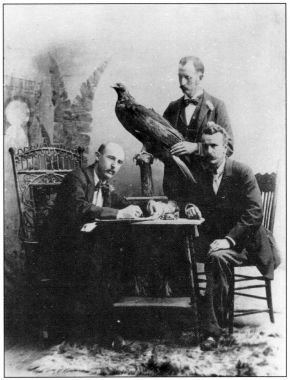

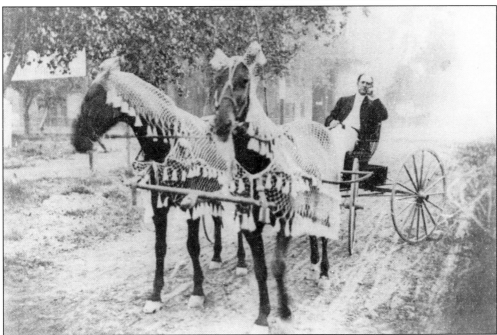

W. L. Bobo, a Carlsbad schoolteacher, takes his buggy out with his matching pair of horses in fly net livery. The netting not only kept flies off the horses, but provided observers with a fanciful sight. Bobo is driving his rig on Mermod Street near the corner of Canal Street, and the Tansill building can be seen in the background.

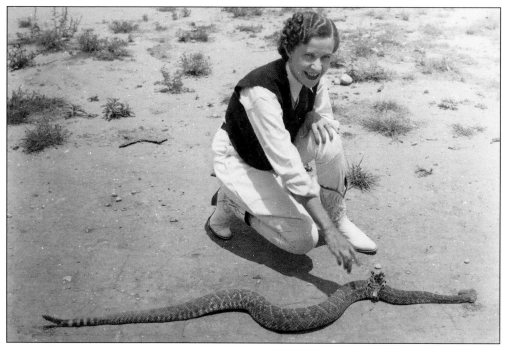

Gracie Campbell points out the tiny saddle strapped to the back of a diamondback rattlesnake in a promotional photograph for the Rattlesnake Derby. A prize of $500 would go to the person who held the number of a wire wicket that the rattlesnake crawled through first. It is reported that the first derby, complete with wagering, was organized by local women as a fund-raiser.

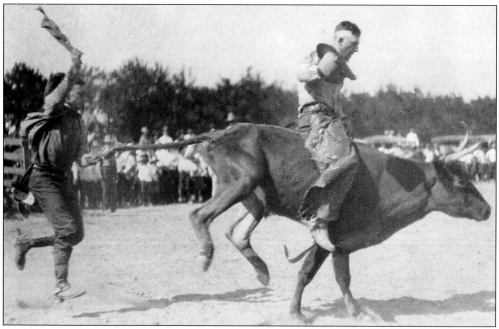

A rodeo clown twists the tail of Charlie Hepler's wild steer in a 1926 event. Charlie Hepler and his brothers were avid horsemen, developing a quarter horse racing stable which housed Shue Fly, the world champion quarter horse three years running. Shue Fly had an AAA top speed rating.

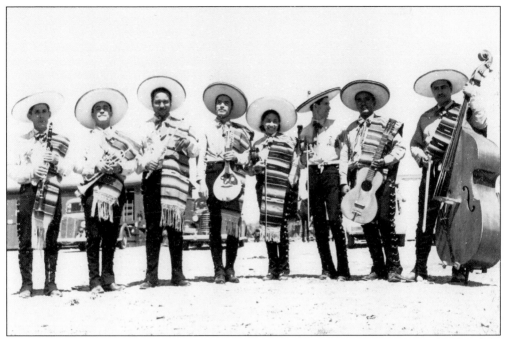

Mariachi bands, such as the one shown in this 1942 photograph at the James Ranch, played for rodeos, dances, and parades, bringing a taste of the vibrant Hispanic culture in Carlsbad for everyone to enjoy. Colorfully dressed, the band would roam the streets and restaurants, or play for the twirling dancers along the parade route, much to the delight of all who heard their lively music.

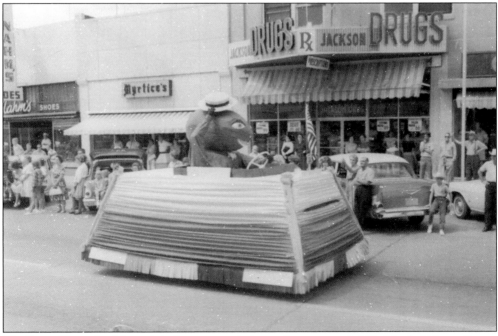

The Pecan Festival celebrated the huge pecan industry that surrounded Carlsbad. A Pecan Queen and her court chosen from the descendants of pioneer families presided over the festivities. A parade featuring the Mr. Nut pecan float, shown here, was a highlight of the weeklong event.

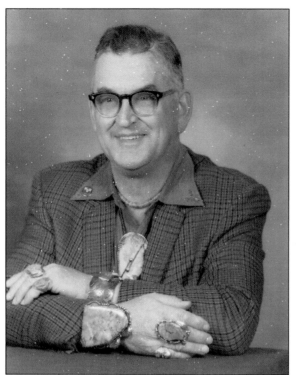

"Turquoise Kid" William Balgemann, an amateur archaeologist, naturalist, and historian, amassed several file cabinets full of invaluable, pertinent information about early Carlsbad people. His love for turquoise was evident in the amount of jewelry featuring the stone he wore. Balgemann worked in the potash industry for years before accepting a job with the Living Desert State Park as their resident caretaker.

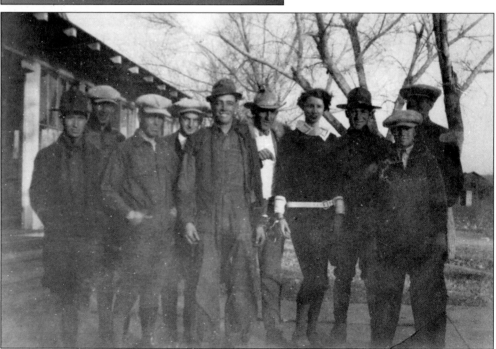

A 1924 photograph of newlyweds, Roy Forehand and Massie Forgham, shows the tradition of handcuffing a newly married couple together and taking them 12 miles out in the middle of nowhere, in separate locations, and having them find their way back home as a prank. Roy Forehand was a member of the fire department and National Guard.

Frank Kindel is pictured on his unicycle, which he rode regularly for parades or just around town. Known for being a daredevil, Kindel rode his motorcycle across the top of the concrete flume at the request of the Warner News Organization. He was known as Carlsbad's "Mr. Welcome" and owned the Sweet Shop in downtown.

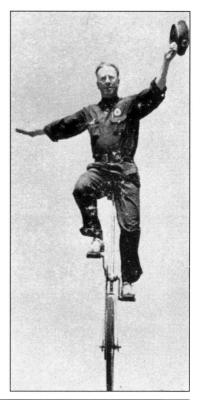

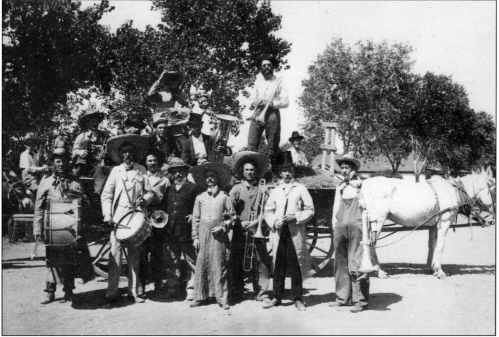

The Hayseed Band, which included an elderly Robert Tansill on the cymbals, was a group of amateurs who gathered together as a spoof of a hillbilly band for a parade in 1906. Tansill's willingness to join the young people was remarkable and brought humor to the one-time group.

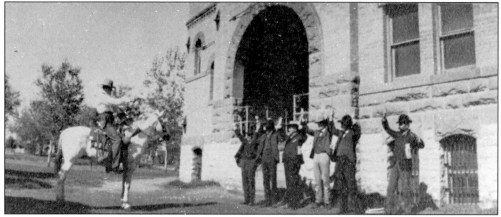

On his white horse, sheriff Cicero Stewart holds the Courthouse Gang at bay in this tongue-in-cheek photograph taken in front of the first Eddy County Courthouse. The courthouse was built in the Victorian style of the times on land donated by Charles Eddy, and was later redone in a Pueblo style.

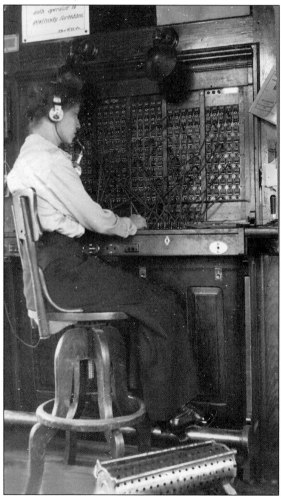

Frona Leck is shown manning the switchboard in 1912 at Carlsbad's central Public Utilities Telephone Service office. Carlsbad originally had 600 phone numbers, which rapidly increased in a few short years.

Abel Justus Crawford, shown here in 1910, was a sheepherder, businessman, and banker. Crawford started his career as a sheepherder in Runnels County, Texas, and later moved to Eddy County to start his own herd. He married Minnie Campbell in 1898, and the couple settled in Carlsbad. There he founded the Crawford Hotel and People's Mercantile chains, and originated the First National Bank with H. J. Hammond.

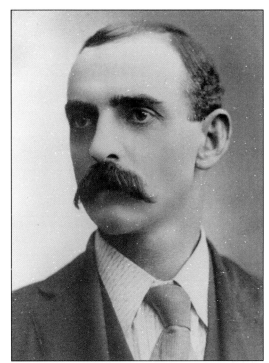

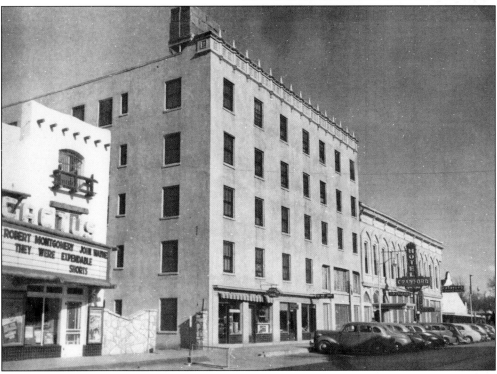

The 28-room Crawford Hotel, which opened with a formal banquet on November 28, 1917, was proud to be the first hotel in the state to be truly air conditioned. The Crawford Hotel later increased in size to 116 rooms and boasted being one of the most modern hotels in the state.

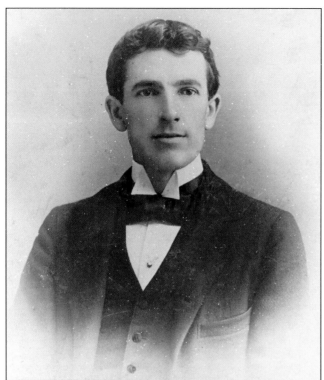

Etienne P. Bujac, shown here in 1898, was a Carlsbad attorney and orator extraordinaire who was said to have the ability of reducing his opponent in court to tears. He had a highly decorated military career during which he received the Congressional Medal of Honor. As a legal advocate for the Hispanic and black communities, he would often provide pro bono legal services. He was the father of actor Bruce Cabot.

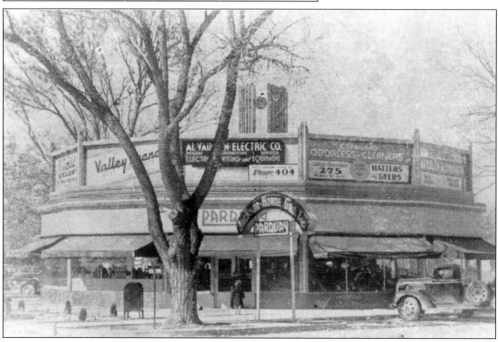

The 12-sided Jackson-Horne Grocery Store on north Canal Street had no corners. The wide display windows, each covered with an awning, provided people with views of the store from every direction. When the 12 neon lighted signboards on top of the building were illuminated, it gave the effect of having a revolving top.

108

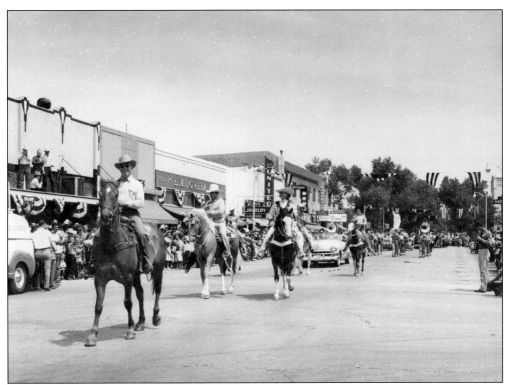

Rodeo parades featuring the Eddy County Sheriff's Posse were a favorite summertime event, as shown in this 1949 photograph. The Posse would perform synchronized maneuvers along the parade route that looked much like a square dance on horseback. Sharply dressed and with each horse wearing turquoise saddle blankets, they never failed to thrill.

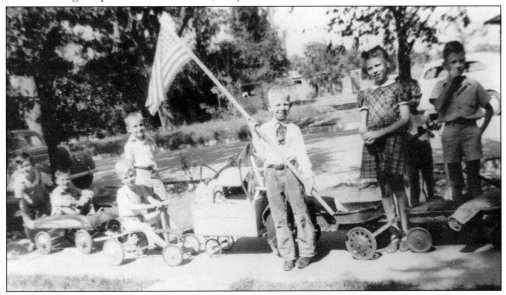

A group of patriotic children organized their own sidewalk parade. Peddle cars, tricycles, and little red wagons were featured in the impromptu festivities. The group's leader proudly displays a child-sized American flag. Civic pride started early in Carlsbad.

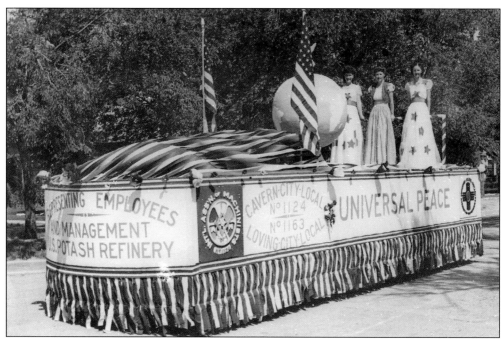

The Potash Company of America's 1946 Labor Day float is pictured here. Ham Martin, who worked at the potash mine and later became mayor, would spend all year designing and building elaborate floats to present in the many parades Carlsbad had throughout the year. Countless boxes of tissues, endless yards of crepe paper, and many rolls of chicken wire were used to construct these beautiful floats each year.

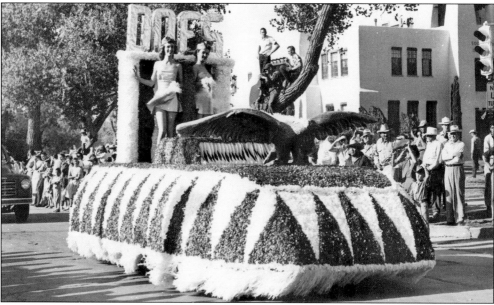

The 1951 ELKS/DOES float pays tribute to American freedom. The streets are lined with some of the same 6,000 cottonwood trees planted in 1889. The Eddy County Courthouse, which was converted to a Pueblo styling in 1939 from its original Victorian design of 1914, can be seen in the background. Charles Eddy gave the land and the $40,000 needed to build the first courthouse.

Nine

GENTLE TOUCH

As the adage goes, the west was hard on horses and even harder on women. Being raised with refinements made the hardships women faced in their new lives in New Mexico Territory much more difficult. Pioneer woman had to be strong, sometimes much stronger, than their male counterparts to survive a hard land where everything seemed to have thorns.

Women softened the edges for the men. They tended to the affairs of the home, nurtured a community out of a group of buildings, started hospitals, schools, and libraries, tended the sick who sought a cure in the dry climate, and developed culture as sponsors of the arts.

It was not only the gentle women who formed the community; it was also the farmers' and ranchers' wives who worked long arduous days beside her husbands to provide a living for their families. Unmarried women and widows forged their own ways, many times going against the grain to complete projects a woman was not considered to be able to accomplish. Even the women everyone only whispered about, the ladies of Phenix, played a part in the development of early Carlsbad.

The women of recent Carlsbad have held up the tradition well. Doctors, judges, school superintendents, artists, businesswomen, actresses, journalists, and activists are but a few of the positions held by present-day women. Each Carlsbad woman has left her mark on the community, forming it into the modern city it is today.

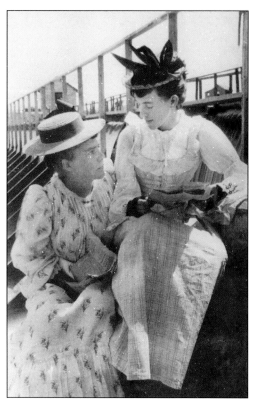

Olive Clark (the future Mrs. Francis G. Tracy), in the feathered hat, and her friend Myra Emmons enjoy the newspaper at the Spillway of Avalon Dam in 1894. Tracy spearheaded the development of the hospital and library. She donated the first book to the library, which is still in the collection, and founded the Women's Club, a driving force in the community.

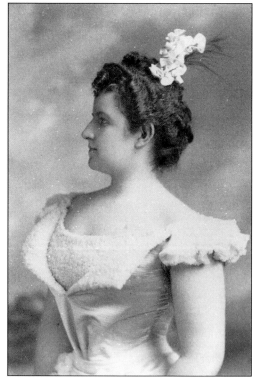

Tubercular patient Cesarine Graves, shown here in her coming out portrait at age 16, moved with her sisters to Eddy for the dry climate. She later became one of the wealthiest women in Carlsbad, and was generous to the town by giving them the land along the river known as the Beach. The land was given as long as it remained free of charge to the people.

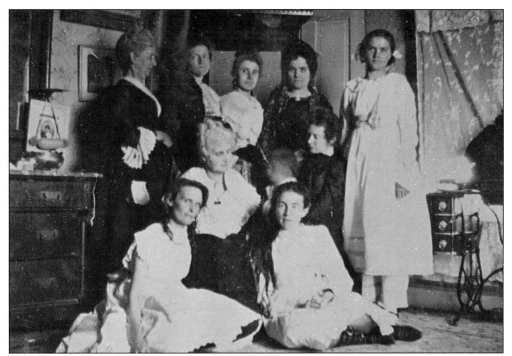

This photograph was taken at the Women's Club costume party on February 22, 1900. Attending the party were Aggie Farrell, Mrs. Skeats, Rose Stone, Jennie Pratt, Mrs. Spencer, Olive Tracy, Antoinette Christian, Mrs. Miller, and Mrs. Freeman. These ladies represented many of the most influential families in the Pecos Valley at this time.

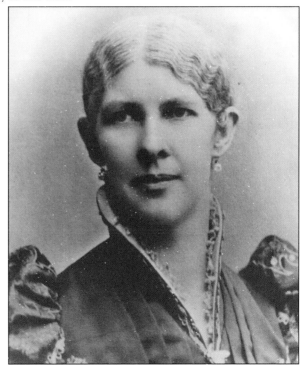

Anna Hex Hagerman, pictured here in 1890, stood by her husband through all of his many business ventures, but did not want him to invest with Charles B. Eddy. She considered Eddy a Svengali, and blamed him for all of their later money losses, encouraging her husband to leave the Pecos Valley area.

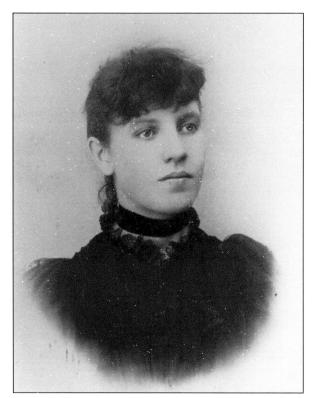

Ida Woodward came to Eddy in 1889 as a piano teacher, but upon finding no pianos in the area, she left to teach school in a small settlement 12 miles north of Eddy, named Seven Rivers. She returned to Eddy when pianos began to arrive with new settler families.

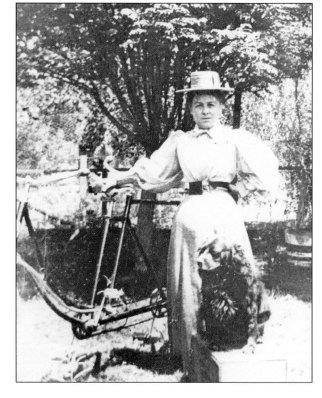

Edith Ohl, pictured here with her bicycle built for two in 1890, was the first paid schoolteacher in Eddy. A $2,000, one-room adobe schoolhouse built by the Pecos Valley Town Company provided Ohl and her students with a place to learn the three Rs. On one occasion, after the schoolhouse was used for an election and the use of chewing tobacco on the premesis was apparent the next morning, Ohl lectured the children on its vices.

Barbara "Ma'am" Jones in 1897 was the picture of a strong woman, put to the test on many occasions as the mother of eight boys and one girl. As one of the few persons with nursing knowledge in the violent town of Seven Rivers, Jones was called upon frequently to administer to the citizens, including Billy the Kid, who once showed up shoeless at her door.

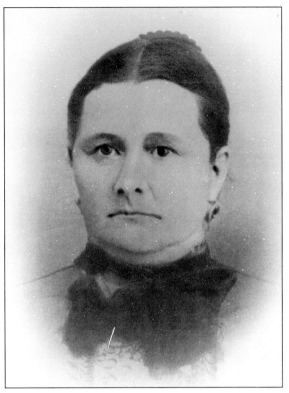

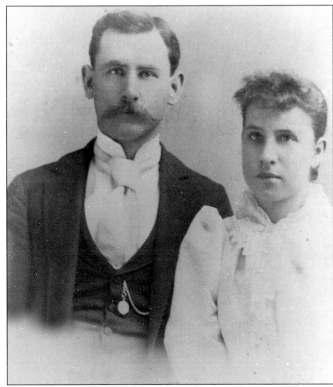

Flora Ryan, longtime librarian of the Carlsbad Public Library, was elected librarian in May 1929 and continued in the job until June 1952. Quick-witted, she was known to make terse statements that drove to the heart of a matter. When new patrons offered advice and criticism, she would shake her finger at them and reply, "You read the books. I'll run the library."

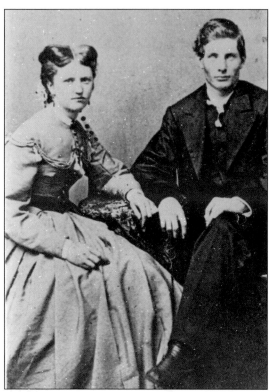

Lucius Anderson and his wife Josephine were two of the few people to come to Eddy from the west. The couple, originally from San Francisco, moved to Tombstone, Arizona before finally settling in Eddy. While here, the Andersons opened a tuberculosis sanitarium in their home before building a two-story adobe building to house their many patients. Josephine was known as the Angel of the Pecos.

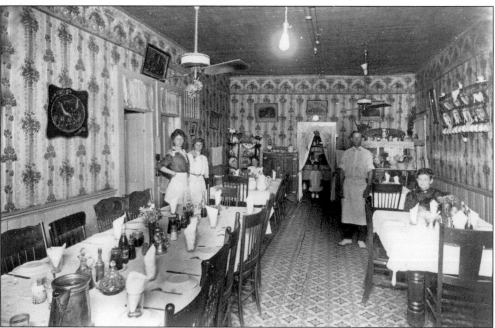

The interior of the dining room of the Anderson Sanitarium is pictured in 1897. The adobe structure, located at the northwest corner of Shaw and Main Streets, was the biggest in town. The dining facilities were only available to the tubercular patients of the Anderson Sanitarium. Josephine Anderson tirelessly provided care to both tubercular and Spanish influenza patients.

Dr. Myrtle D. Harkey was the first woman chiropractor in Carlsbad. A pioneer in the field, she opened her practice in 1895. The daughter of famed lawman Daniel R. "Dee" Harkey, Dr. Harkey was well known in town and remained here until her death. She never married.

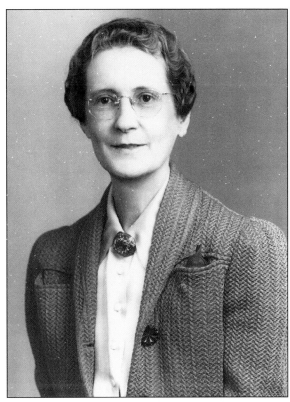

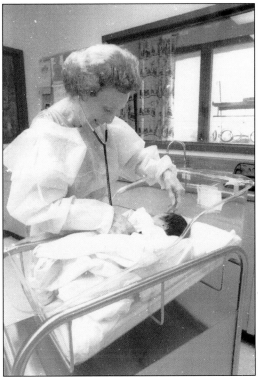

Dr. Catherine Armstrong was Carlsbad's first pediatrician in 1950. Catherine received her medical degree from Chicago University in 1942, where she met her husband John Seward. He did not approve of her practicing medicine, so when he went off to World War II, she moved to Carlsbad with her son. Known as a tough doctor, often telling mothers exactly what she thought, her patients were always her first priority.

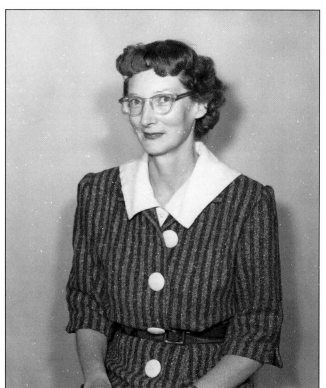

A huge benefactor of the arts, Frances Feezer spent her life promoting and supporting the Carlsbad Museum and Art Center and many other organizations in Carlsbad. Gov. Bill Richardson honored her in 2003 with the Governor's Art Award, New Mexico's most prestigious artistic honor, for her individual support of the Carlsbad Museum.

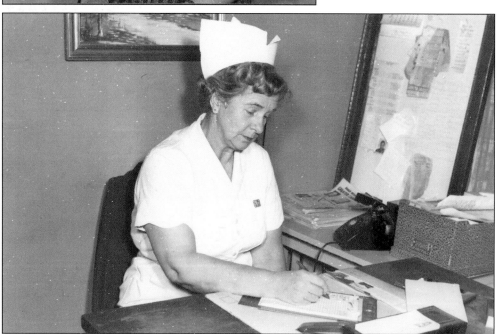

The Neighborhood House was spoken about in hushed tones. Virginia Fawcett, a registered nurse, came to Carlsbad in 1960 and immediately saw a need for birth control among the poor of the town. Fawcett was not accepted by society for her work, a subject no one wanted to address at the time, but did not let that disrupt her mission.

The St. Francis Hospital, situated across the street from St. Edward's Church, was run by the Sisters of the Adorers of the Blood of Christ. Sister Mary Benedict was head of pediatrics and is credited with saving over 5,000 babies during her career, including the author. She became known as a miracle worker in many circles; when it seemed nothing could be done, Sister Mary Benedict would find a way.

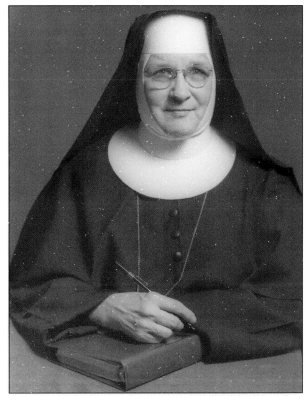

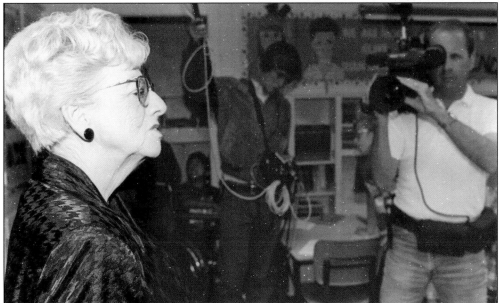

Lynn Pitcaithley demonstrates tireless efforts on behalf of the stray animals of Carlsbad. She developed a highly popular program where people received a certificate to spay or neuter a pet in exchange for a $10 donation, thus preventing untold numbers of unwanted births. A professional Vaudeville actress, she and her husband came to Carlsbad during World War II, where she continued on the stage for the community theater.

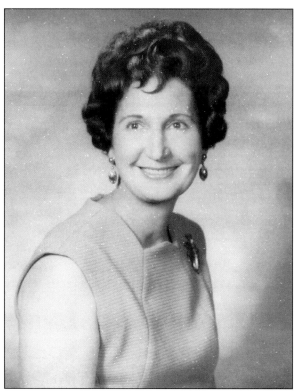

A great promoter of literacy, Ann Wood was asked to be the first program coordinator of the Carlsbad Literacy Program in 1985. The program provides tutoring and educational help at no charge for individuals who are not able to read or write. The Ann Wood Literacy Center was dedicated in 1996 after her death.

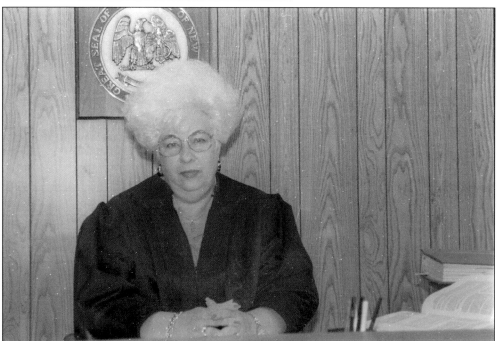

Nancy Beard retired from the bench as magistrate judge in 1994, a position she had held since 1983. She is known for her quick wit and good humor. As a member of a pioneer family dating back to 1898 who established the Grapevine Spring Ranch, Beard is proud of her Carlsbad roots.

A formidable force in the community, Sarah Jackson could only be described as a mover and shaker. Starting the local chapter of the Daughters of the American Revolution, Jackson represented Carlsbad in Washington, D.C. in 1976 during the United States centennial celebrations. Serving as the president of the library board, she guided the library through several decades until her death.

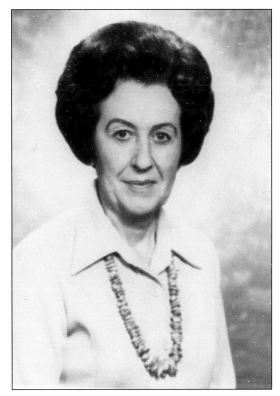

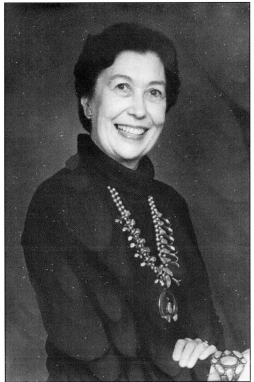

Winnie Van Cleave is credited with starting the Carlsbad (NM) Aware Program sponsored by the United Way in 1979. The program promotes knowledge and understanding about teen issues, in particular teenage pregnancy. As the result of her efforts, special classrooms and educational programs have been established to allow pregnant teens to complete their education.

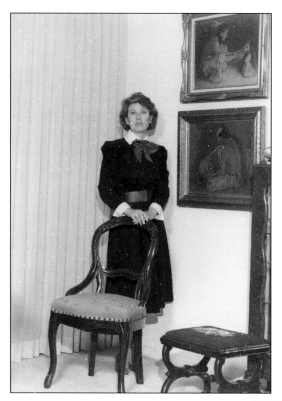

With nearly 30 years of legal experience, Jane Shuler Gray was appointed by Gov. Bill Richardson as a judge on New Mexico's Fifth Judicial District Court in Carlsbad. Known for her outstanding character and integrity, the Carlsbad native has had involvement with family, commercial, and criminal law, and is also a registered nurse.

A civic-minded dynamo, Janell Whitlock has served her community as municipal judge for 18 years, an Eddy County commissioner for four years, and as the director of retirement for the Carlsbad Chamber of Commerce. In 1996, Whitlock was awarded the New Mexico Commission on the Status of Women Governors Award for Outstanding Women. She helped organize the New Mexico Municipal Court Clerks Association and served as its first president.

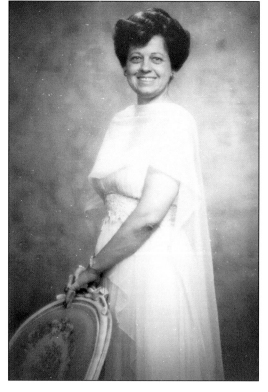

A driving force in the black community, Minner Crockett has been vital to bringing much-needed awareness of black history to Carlsbad. She was instrumental in securing funding to establish the Martin Luther King Jr. Memorial Park, and is also known for her many years as a police dispatcher and artist.

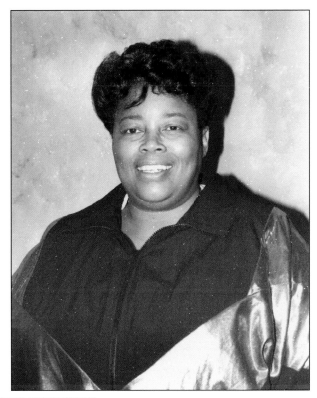

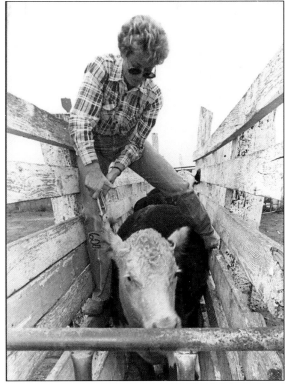

Alisa Ogden, president of the New Mexico Cattle Grower's Association, was recently presented with the *Restore New Mexico* award for her efforts in grassland preservation on the ranches that have been in her family since 1918. Ogden is a hands-on ranch hand and an outstanding promoter of the ranching way of life.

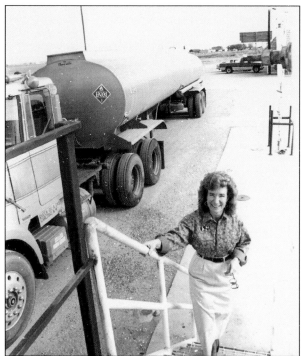

Dorothy Queen and her husband formed oil and gas operations from the ground up, and she took over after his death. Queen is a large supporter of the arts and believes in the immediate need for water conservation. Her biggest risk was changing the course of her business, which she has done well as being one of the five largest female-owned businesses in the state.

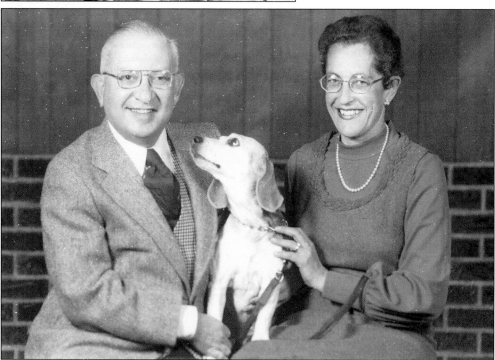

Irene Goldminz-Roberts, shown here with her late husband Abraham and their beagle Gum-Gum, is credited with establishing the first Jewish temple in Carlsbad. She continues her work by serving as treasurer for the congregation. As a nurse, she is concerned with health, and has donated heavily to improve the health of sufferers of chronic and life-threatening illnesses.

Sculptor Wren Prather-Stroud, a former Miss New Mexico, works as manager for the Center of Excellence for Hazardous Materials Management, which is attempting to produce biodiesel from algae. In 1997, Wren completed a commissioned larger-than-life bronze sculpture to commemorate the library's centennial.

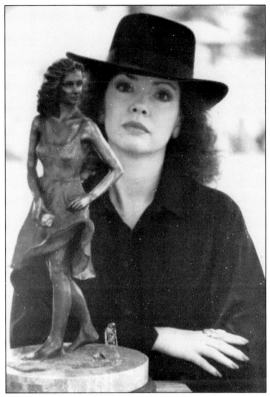

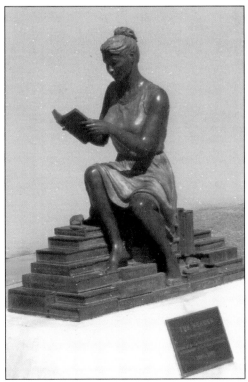

Prather-Stroud's sculpture *The Reader* adorns the entrance to the Carlsbad Public Library and promotes reading. *The Reader* sits on a stack of books with titles meaningful to the Carlsbad community and to the artist, and holds *The Leaves of Grass* by Walt Whitman.

125

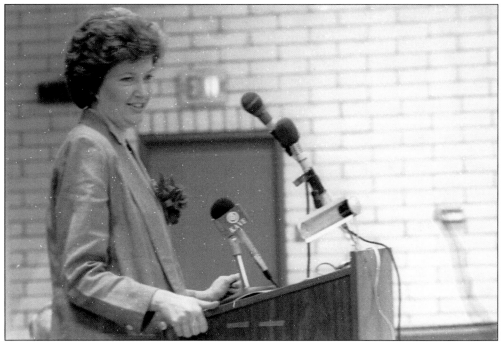

Linda Wertheimer, a Carlsbad native, entered into journalism after graduating from Wellesley College in 1965. She was the first woman to anchor National Public Radio's coverage of a presidential nomination and election night, and as of 2008, she has anchored ten election nights. Since she started as host for the radio show *All Things Considered*, record numbers have tuned in.

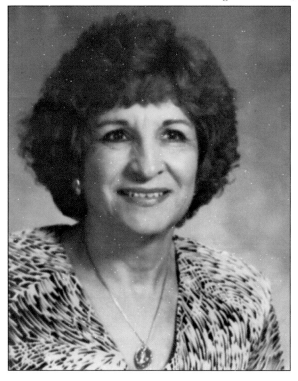

Refugia "Cuca" Castillo received her doctorate of education in curriculum and instruction from New Mexico State University in 1997. Castillo has been a prominent member of the League of United Latin American Citizens and a member of the Carlsbad Museum and Art Center board. She was given the honor of woman of the year by the Business and Professional Women in 2000.

BIBLIOGRAPHY

Bogener, Stephen. *Ditches Across the Desert: Irrigation in the Lower Pecos Valley.* Lubbock, TX: Texas Tech University Press, 2003.

Burns, Terry. *History of the Carlsbad Chamber of Commerce, 1891–1991.* Carlsbad, NM: Carlsbad Chamber of Commerce, 1992.

Eddy County, New Mexico to 1981. Carlsbad, NM: Southeastern New Mexico Historical Society, 1982.

Howard, Jed. *Phenix and the Wolf: The Saloon Battles of Eddy and the David Kemp Saga, A Summary of the Contemporary Newspaper Accounts.* Carlsbad, NM: Southeastern New Mexico Historical Society, 1999.

Hufstetler, Mark and Lon Johnson. *Watering the Land: The Turbulent History of the Carlsbad Irrigation District.* Denver, CO: National Park Service, Rocky Mountain Region, Division of National Preservation Programs, 1993.

Myers, Lee C. *The Pearl of the Pecos: The Story of the Establishment of Eddy, New Mexico, and Irrigation on the Lower Pecos River of New Mexico, Complied from Eddy Newspapers between October 12, 1889, and October 23, 1897.* Carlsbad, NM: Southeastern New Mexico Historical Society, 1999.

Pageant of Progress. Historical souvenir program. Carlsbad, NM: Carlsbad Diamond Jubilee, 1963.

Ryan, Flora. *History of Carlsbad, New Mexico: Complied by the Carlsbad Public Library for the Students of the Carlsbad Public Schools.* Carlsbad, NM: Carlsbad Public Library, 1947.

DISCOVER THOUSANDS OF LOCAL HISTORY BOOKS
FEATURING MILLIONS OF VINTAGE IMAGES

Arcadia Publishing, the leading local history publisher in the United States, is committed to making history accessible and meaningful through publishing books that celebrate and preserve the heritage of America's people and places.

Find more books like this at
www.arcadiapublishing.com

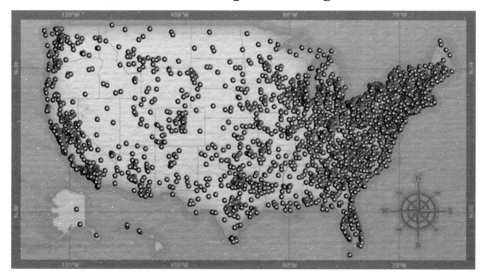

Search for your hometown history, your old stomping grounds, and even your favorite sports team.

Consistent with our mission to preserve history on a local level, this book was printed in South Carolina on American-made paper and manufactured entirely in the United States. Products carrying the accredited Forest Stewardship Council (FSC) label are printed on 100 percent FSC-certified paper.

MADE IN THE 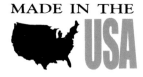 USA